MARRIAGE AS AN ECONOMIC PARTNERSHIP

Marriage as an Economic Partnership

How One State Made It Happen

JOSEPHINE HELEN STAAB

ATWOOD PUBLISHING
Madison, Wisconsin : : 1998

LIBRARY OF CONGRESS CATALOGING-IN-PUBLICATION DATA

Staab, Jo.
    Marriage as an economic partnership : how one state made
it happen / Josephine Helen Staab. — 1st ed.
       p.   cm.
    Includes index.
    ISBN 1-891859-26-9 (alk. paper)
      1. Marital property—Wisconsin—History.   I. Title.
KFW2497.S73 1998
346.77501'66—dc21   98-24535
                                             CIP

ISBN 1-891859-26-9

Printed in the United States of America on recycled paper.

The paper used in this publication meets the minimum requirements
of the American National Standards for Information Sciences—
Permanence of Paper for Printed Library Materials, ANSI Z39.48-1984.

Designed and typeset by Gregory M. Britton.

Published by
ATWOOD PUBLISHING
P. O. Box 3185
Madison, Wisconsin
53704

FIRST EDITION

To the women and men who made the
Wisconsin Marital Property Act
a reality

Contents

ᴊᴇ PART III

ᴊᴇ APPENDIX

Acknowledgments

THIS BOOK COULD NOT HAVE BEEN written without the encouragement, cooperation, and generosity of people who shared an interest in having a one-volume reference dealing with the property rights of spouses in Wisconsin for persons who are not trained in law. I thank all who read the early drafts of the manuscript for their ideas and constructive criticisms. I thank the reviewers of the final draft, Margaret Monroe, Professor Emerita of Library Science, University of Wisconsin-Madison; Anne Short, a Madison freelance writer; and James Fosdick, Professor Emeritus of Journalism, UW-Extension, for their help and pertinent comments.

I am deeply indebted to June Weisberger, Professor Emerita, Law School, University of Wisconsin-Madison, for reading every draft of the manuscript and checking the correctness of the legal explanation given. I am grateful to her for her patience and commitment to legal accuracy.

I thank Ellen Henningsen, an attorney and former Executive Director, Wisconsin Women's Network, for her support and contributions throughout the writing of this book. I thank Don Dyke, Senior Staff Attorney, Legislative Council for his help on legislative information.

To Gene Boyer, a very special thank you for giving the book its title, and thanks to Greg Britton, director of Madison House Publishers, for his guidance and help in publishing this book.

Josephine H. Staab
Professor Emerita, Family Economics
School of Human Ecology, University of Wisconsin-Madison

Introduction

Marriage as an Economic Partnership: How One State Made It Happen combines a discussion of history and law. Enactment of the Wisconsin Marital Property Act was a legislative achievement of historic proportions. Its passage concluded the transition from a system of law that deprived married women of property rights to a system of law that granted married women the same property rights as married men. How the reform legislation was developed and skillfully engineered through every step of the legislative process is covered in Part I. The detailed legal explanation of the provisions of the Wisconsin Marital Property Act, the current law in Wisconsin governing the property rights of spouses, is covered in Part II, along with an explanation of the history of married women's property rights in Wisconsin. Part III covers the 1998 Amendments to the Probate Code that affect the 1984 Marital Property Act.

When the Territory of Wisconsin was established in 1836, the English common law system was the legal system in force. Rules governing the property rights of spouses were an important part of English common law. The dominant feature of the property rules was the "doctrine of coverture" which meant that when a woman married she lost her legal existence or at least it was suspended during marriage. A married woman was under the protection and coverture of her husband. In the eyes of the law only one person managed the couple's legal affairs, and that person was the husband.

The first fundamental change in the law governing the property rights of spouses was initiated in the Territory of Wisconsin by delegates to the 1846 Convention convened to draft a state constitution. The proposed constitution included Article XIV "On the Rights of Married Women." The article proved to be such a controversial issue, however, that the voters in the Territory of Wisconsin rejected the constitution. (Voters passed a constitution in 1848 resulting in statehood, but it was silent on the rights of married women.) The alternative procedure for changing the property law by legislative action was acceptable to the convention delegates. In 1850, the Wisconsin State Legislature passed a law giving married women the right to own property.

The 1850 Wisconsin law restored the legal existence of married women and rejected or abolished the "doctrine of coverture." The law was amended from time to time to give additional property rights to married women. The Wisconsin Law of 1850 was one of the earliest Married Women's Property Acts passed in the United States. These acts were the beginning of the separate property system, an American legal innovation. Under this property system married women, as well as married men, could own separate property. Removing English common law disabilities imposed on married women was a slow process. In December 1985, the month prior to the effective date of the Marital Property Act, some English common law disabilities of married women still existed in Wisconsin because the state legislature had not specifically removed or repealed them.

The second basic change in the law governing the property rights of spouses was generated by the proposed Equal Rights Amendment to the United States Constitution passed by Congress in 1972. Coupled with the drive to achieve equal rights generally was a commitment to resolve the spousal inequities in the Wisconsin separate property system. In 1984, the state legislature passed and the Governor signed the Marital Property Act giving married women and married men equal and identical property rights. The law became effective on January 1, 1986. (See Chapter 1, "History of the Wisconsin Marital Property Act.")

"Sharing" of income and property acquired during marriage

through the efforts of either or both spouses is the basic underlying principle of the marital property law. Wisconsin is the first and only state in the nation to change by legislative action from a separate property state to a marital property state, a form of community property.

Men took the initiative to make the first fundamental change in Wisconsin property law in 1850 and women took the initiative in the 1970s to bring about the second basic change. The history of the passage of the Marital Property Act is detailed in Part I. Historical perspective on the legal systems that embodied spousal inequities in property law is provided in Chapters 3 and 4 of Part II. Chapter 3 deals with the property rights of spouses under English common law, the legal system in the Territory of Wisconsin. Chapter 4 deals with the property rights of spouses under separate property law, the legal system in the state of Wisconsin from 1850 through 1985. Chapters 5, 6, and 7 of Part II explain the property rights of spouses under the new Wisconsin marital property system, a Wisconsin legal innovation.

Part III covers the 1998 Amendments to the Probate Code that affect the 1984 Marital Property Act. Inclusion of the revisions of the Probate Code means the reader has access to the law in effect through December 31, 1998 and, also, the new substantive changes in the law governing the property rights of spouses in Wisconsin that become effective January 1, 1999. They are explained in Part III.

For the convenience of the reader a section "Explanation of Terms" has been included. For readers interested in pursuing a specific aspect of the Wisconsin Marital Property Act a section on "Selected References" and one on "Notes" have been included. These are followed by the index.

Economic partnership in this book means marriage is a legal contract between two equal persons, husband and wife as defined by Wisconsin law in Chapter 766 of the Wisconsin Statutes. Therefore, economic partnership in this book does *not* mean a legal business partnership contract signed by two or more partners.

This book does *not* give legal advice. The intent is to provide a background and an explanation of the new marital property system that governs the economic rights of spouses during marriage, and their property rights when that marriage ends with the death of a spouse. The background and explanation of the law are current as of January 1, 1999. This book does *not* cover divorce law.

Changing laws governing the legal and economic rights of women by legislative action is a long and slow process with many facets. In Wisconsin the effort to achieve equal rights generally and to remove spousal inequities in the separate property system reinforced each other and evolved into a coherent plan of action. Pioneering in legislative reform required the talents of astute professional women who were willing to take leadership roles in different aspects of the process. Creative thinking, combined with research, produced an original comprehensive marital property legislative reform proposal. Concurrently, a broad-based education program enabled farm, rural, and urban women to recognize their common interest in property law reform. These actions were followed by the development of grassroots political skills, such as advocacy and lobbying. Women legislators sponsored legislative reform proposals and directed legislative strategies to keep the bills "on track" within the legislature. A detailed account of what happened in Wisconsin between 1972 and 1986, is given in Chapter 1, "History of the Wisconsin Marital Property Act." The information is included in this book to give others interested in legislative reform insights into the process and the long-term commitment it takes to achieve success. In many ways Wisconsin may be considered a model for other states seeking equal rights for all of its citizens to reconstruct the legal system governing marital property law.

Part I 🌿

CHAPTER 1 ✍

History of the Wisconsin Marital Property Act

Overview

The Wisconsin 1984 Marital Property Act was a historic legislative achievement. The creative thinking, tireless effort and commitment of women and men of different races and ethnic groups as well as different types of organizations made possible its enactment.

To convey the impression that it was a simple, easy task to replace the separate property system with a marital property system would be a disservice.

Between 1972 and 1986, an unusual set of circumstances and unexpected events interacted to create opportunities for women to fill leadership roles in Wisconsin. There was a pool of well-educated, experienced, and astute women available and willing to assume these roles. The saga of the Wisconsin Marital Property Act portrays these women working together to achieve a common goal.

In the Territory of Wisconsin at the 1846 Constitutional Convention, one of the public policy issues addressed by the delegates was the property rights of married women. The men who took the initiative to change the property rules achieved their goal in 1850 when the state Legislature enacted a Wisconsin version of the Married Women's Property Act. In 1972, women, with male allies, took the initiative to change the law governing the property rights of spouses. The women realized that it would take time to educate the voters on the nature of the public policy issue and to develop a reform proposal on the property rights of spouses that the legislature would consider seriously. The women also recognized that the political process of enacting reform legislation required strong grassroots support to convince the state legislators that the proposed legislative change was endorsed by the majority of the people.

Most public policy issues are controversial. They generate adversaries, those in favor of change and those who oppose it. Only time and effort can answer the question: "Who will be the winner?"

The framework for reporting what, how, and why things happened in Wisconsin in the 1970s and 1980s consists of three phases: 1) Discovery of a Public Policy Issue; 2) A Kaleidoscope of Events Associated with Wisconsin Marital Property Reform; 3) Legislative History of Reform Proposals. Each phase is a story in itself where the plot, the actors, and the action unfold. The time span of Phase I is 1972–1979. The concurrent time span for Phase II and Phase III is 1979–1986. A pattern of sequential developments within each subject covered was chosen to give the reader a relatively detailed and complete account of that subject. In Phase II, this pattern of presentation makes some abrupt shifts in the subject being reported. Occasionally the reader may need to pause and reflect on how the diverse elements of history are linked together and collectively shaped the Wisconsin Marital Property Act and its enactment by the Wisconsin Legislature.

Phase I: Discovery of a Public Policy Issue

Two movements concerned with the economic and legal position of women, one at the state, the other at the national level, converged in Wisconsin in the 1970s. The interaction of these movements clarified the public policy issue—the need to remove the inequities in the separate property law governing the property rights of spouses during marriage and when that marriage ends with the death of a spouse.

Governor's Commission on the Status of Women

The Governor's Commission on the Status of Women was created by Executive Order of Governor John Reynolds in 1964. It was established in response to an "invitation to action" issued to the states in the 1963 report of the President's Commission on the Status of Women. The charge of the Commission was to investigate all aspects of the lives of women, with a view to improving their status and widening their opportunity for full participation in the life of our times. The thirty-seven member Commission was composed of women and men.

Co-directors of "Women in Apprenticeship," a three year research project, 1970–1973, were Kathryn Clarenbach, Chair of the Governor's Commission on the Status of Women, and Charlie Nye, Head of Apprenticeship Programs in the Wisconsin Department of Industry, Labor and Human Services. The question addressed was: "Why were so few women in traditionally male blue-collar, skilled trades?" (Electricians, plumbers, etc.) Norma Briggs was hired to work on the research and demonstration project. As a result of this project, a second research project was developed to analyze the difference in skill levels attributed to traditionally male versus traditionally female occupations that were rated in the "Dictionary of Occupational Titles." The findings of this research revealed that "homemaker" was not even listed as an occupation. Only jobs in the marketplace that pay a wage or salary were listed in the "Dictionary of Occupational Titles."

In the "World of Work," where the size of one's salary is an indication of the importance of an occupation, the unpaid full-time homemaker who received no money for her work had no occupational standing or merit. In addition to this demeaning view of a homemaker's occupational status, the separate property system in Wisconsin assigned an economic value of zero to the

unpaid work of the full-time homemaker. By contrast, the opponents of the Equal Rights Amendments, both national and state,
declared that the work of the full-time homemaker in the home
for the benefit of the family was an occupation of the highest
order that should be preserved at all costs. Women were encouraged to fulfill themselves as mothers and homemakers (in the
home) because that was where they belonged and where their
contributions were valued by society. The "myth" was that good
women were rewarded for this approved and conventional choice.

The Commission operated without state funding from 1964
to 1973. Kathryn Clarenbach, Professor of Women's Education
Resources and Family Living, UW-Extension, Madison, was the
Chair of the Governor's Commission on the Status of Women
from its creation in 1964 to its termination in 1979. She explained
how the Commission coped with the situation:

> . . . My University office doubled as the Commission head-
> quarters. Appointed Chair of the Commission by Governors
> Reynolds, Knowles, Lucy and Schreiber and with the blessings
> of University administrators, I was able to use desk, phone,
> secretary, time and occasionally even travel funds for Com-
> mission business. The location of Commission leadership
> within the University exemplified the Wisconsin Idea. The re-
> sources of the University were familiar and accessible, and with
> the mission of my University assignment consistent with the
> goals of the Commission, both programs were enriched. There
> is no question but that the strength of Wisconsin's Commission
> and its key role in the evolution of the Wisconsin Women's
> Movement are directly attributable to its base in the University.
> The development of our agenda, the quality of our publica-
> tions and conferences, our constant focus on public education
> to broaden and enlighten a sympathetic constituency, all had
> the invaluable underpinning of solid information from a grow-
> ing range of disciplines.[1]

Funding for the Governor's Commission on the Status of
Women in 1973, although limited in amount, was a giant step
forward. It represented a new level of state commitment to the
Commission and provided it with an opportunity to exert its

influence. An Executive Secretary was hired. Norma Briggs held the position from 1973 to June 30, 1979, when the Commission was terminated. The Executive Secretary was responsible for the outreach program, which included producing written informational materials, speaking upon request to different types of organizations, as well as keeping the Commission members informed on issues and events. The Executive Secretary was also responsible for preparing educational materials and organizing workshops and conferences in different parts of the state.

In 1973, the Governor's Commission on the Status of Women wished to demonstrate that it was interested in the problems of all women in Wisconsin, including the full-time homemaker, and not exclusively interested in the problems of women in paid employment.

The Commission was also challenged by the opponents of the Equal Rights Amendment at both the state and national level, who argued that equal rights would destroy the traditional role of married women as wife, mother, and full-time homemaker. They claimed that "feminists" were trying to ruin the family structure by encouraging married women to seek employment outside the home, and thus irretrievably damage family values. To avoid the negative, stereotype label attached to "feminists" as unfeminine, careerists interested only in paid employment whose values were inimical to family values, and to fulfill its commitment to all Wisconsin women, the Commission decided to draw attention to the economic and legal position of married women who fulfilled the traditional role of wife, mother, and full-time homemaker.

In 1974, six conferences on "Homemaking and the Family: Changing Values and Concerns" were held throughout the state. The participants described the inequities of the law governing the property rights of spouses which they had experienced as married women and the impact of these economic hardships on their lives. A full-time homemaker had no independent credit rating of her own; and after years of childraising, she might not even share in the couple's property at the death of her husband. In fact, the full-time homemaker had no legal property rights based on fulfilling that role in Wisconsin, a separate property state, because the wage earner, the husband, was the sole owner of his earnings and had the exclusive right to manage and control his property. The extent and magnitude of these inequities were a startling revelation. They were previously unknown and unrecognized. As a result of the Conference findings, the Governor's Commission made a commitment to study current laws and to work for legislative reform proposals to resolve the inequities in the law governing the property rights of spouses during marriage and when that marriage ends with the death of a spouse or divorce.

Proposed Equal Rights Amendments

An Equal Rights Amendment to the Wisconsin Constitution was passed by two consecutive sessions of the Wisconsin Legislature in 1971 and 1973. On April 3, 1973, the Wisconsin electorate rejected the Equal Rights Amendment to the Wisconsin Constitution by a vote of 447,240 to 520,936. The defeat of the referendum on the amendment was completely unexpected.

Representative Marjorie "Midge" Miller, (D-Madison), Chair of the Assembly Equal Rights Committee, authored the Wisconsin resolution to ratify the Equal Rights Amendment to the United States Constitution. It was passed by Congress on March 22, 1972. In a special session of the legislature, Wisconsin ratified the amendment on April 20, 1972. Wisconsin was the fifteenth state to ratify the Equal Rights Amendment.

In 1972, the Wisconsin legislature anticipated voter approval of the Equal Rights Amendment to the Wisconsin Constitution and ratification of the Equal Rights Amendment to the United States Constitution by three-fourths of the states. This optimism prompted the legislature to initiate the review process of state statutes to implement the anticipated new amendments. In 1972, the legislature directed the Legislative Council to study Wisconsin statutes that differentiated on the basis of sex and to recommend changes that would provide equal protection under the law for both women and men.

The Legislative Council made a report to the legislature for the Special Committee on Equal Rights on February 28, 1973. The report identified 280 statutory provisions that treated women and men differently. To remedy these inequities, a comprehensive bill (referred to as an "omnibus bill" because it consists of a number of miscellaneous provisions) was needed.

1973 Assembly Bill 23, the "omnibus bill," authored by Representative Miller mandated the removal of sexually discriminatory language from the state statutes. The Assembly passed AB 23, but the Senate failed to pass it when its most vocal opponent, Senator Gordon Roseleip, (R-Platteville), held the bill in committee on the basis that the electorate had failed to approve the Equal Rights Amendment to the Wisconsin Constitution.

1975 Assembly Bill 431, a revised version of the 1973 Assembly Bill 23, authored by Representative Miller mandated the removal of sexually discriminatory language from the state statutes in all areas of law except sexual assault, divorce and property rights of spouses during marriage. These three areas of law were excluded because the sponsors of the "omnibus bill" believed there was a need to examine more thoroughly the basic principles in each of these areas of law before proposals for reform could be developed.

1975 Assembly Bill 431 was passed by the legislature on September 26, 1975. Chapter 94, Laws of 1975—"An Act . . . relating to eliminating from the statutes distinctions between persons based on sex" contains the provisions of the "omnibus bill." It is sometimes called the 1975 Wisconsin Equal Rights Act.

The Governor's Commission on the Status of Women took the leadership role in legislative reform and followed through by pressuring the legislature to deal with the areas of law excluded from the "omnibus bill." The first achievement was enactment of Senate Bill 255, a comprehensive statute on sexual assault. Chapter 184, Laws of 1975, is a landmark piece of legislation that defines four degrees of sexual assault. It focuses on the nature of the coercion employed by the assailant rather than on the degree of resistance shown by the victim. The law became effective in 1976.

A simple "no-fault" divorce proposal was considered by the

legislature in 1975. Members of the Governor's Commission, who were advocates of women's issues, urged Representative Mary Lou Munts, (D-Madison), who was completing her law degree, to take responsibility for the development of a broader divorce reform proposal. The Uniform Marriage and Divorce Act adopted in 1970 by the National Conference of Commissioners on Uniform State Laws provided a model law. Assembly Bill 995, a comprehensive divorce reform bill introduced in 1975, was a meld of the Uniform Marriage and Divorce Act and additional provisions designed to protect the nonwage earning spouse in the context of a "no-fault" system. The bill was sponsored in the Assembly by Representative Munts, and in the Senate by Senator Kathryn Morrison, (D-Platteville). This comprehensive divorce reform bill, AB 995, was not reported out of committee in the Assembly. Efforts to amend the simple no-fault bill were ruled not germane. The simple no-fault bill was blocked in the Senate by Senator Morrison and Senator Carl Thompson, (D-Stoughton). This action gave an opportunity for the comprehensive bill to be introduced in the next legislative session. Assembly Bill 100, the comprehensive divorce reform bill, was introduced in 1977. It was enacted by the legislature as Chapter 105, Laws of 1977. The law became effective in 1978. Chapter 767 of the Wisconsin Statutes entitled "Actions Affecting the Family" contains the law governing divorce, legal separation, and annulment.

The 1977 Divorce Reform Act introduced into Wisconsin law the presumption that at divorce property generated by the marital partnership should be divided equally; and, for the first time in Wisconsin, the law recognized the contributions of the nonwage earning spouse and the wage earning spouse as equal in economic value. Although the term "marital property" is not expressly used in the legislation, "marital property" is the common law property term often used to denote property that is *subject to division at divorce* in states with a property system based on English common law. In Wisconsin, property that is subject to division at divorce is properly called "divisible property," *not* "marital property." The latter term is used in Wisconson *only* for property which is owned equally by spouses during marriage and when such ownership rights continue to be recognized when the marriage ends with the death of a spouse.

Development of a Marital Property Legislative Reform Proposal

In the fall of 1975, after the "omnibus bill" was enacted, the Governor's Commission on the Status of Women formed an Ad Hoc Committee composed of legislators, practitioners, law professors, University Extension staff, and representatives of citizen groups such, as the League of Women Voters. The Committee was asked to study alternative legal rules governing spousal property rights and to make tentative policy decisions on what should be included in a legislative reform proposal.

A model state law governing the property rights of spouses during marriage and when that marriage ends with the death of a spouse did *not* exist in 1975. The complexity of the law governing the property rights of spouses and the absence of any clear-cut solutions indicated the need for extensive legal research.

A clinical internship program set up by the University of Wisconsin Law School in cooperation with the Governor's Commission on the Status of Women in 1975, was enlarged to meet the research needs of the Ad Hoc Committee on the law governing the property rights of spouses. Eunice Gibson, a practicing attorney and member of the Governor's Commission, provided on-site supervision of the interns. Professor June Weisberger, who joined the Law School faculty in the fall of 1974, became the director of the internship program in 1976. This launched Professor Weisberger into her major role in the overall supervision of the subsequent 46 drafts of the marital property reform legislative proposals and in the development of amendments to the 1984 Marital Property Act in its implementation phase.

Detailed examination of the statutory law and case law of Wisconsin was initiated to ascertain the status of existing law. The Ad Hoc Committee scrutinized various proposals to amend the separate property system, prepared by the clinical interns who were Law School students. When it became evident that incremental modifications of the separate property system, including legislation based on the Uniform Partnership Act, could not remove the underlying causes for the inequities in the property rights of married women, alternative solutions were sought.

The laws of the eight existing community property states, the laws of the six separate property states that adopted community property legislation primarily for tax reasons for a brief period in the 1940s, and Canadian provincial marital property reform proposals were studied. The alternative solutions researched and reported by the clinical interns were presented to the Ad Hoc Committee. Members of the Committee identified and selected the basic legal concepts essential for genuine reform in the area of property law governing the rights of spouses during marriage and when that marriage ends with the death of a spouse. When the work of the Committee was ready to be incorporated into legislative form in 1978, Representative Mary Lou Munts assumed the leadership role in authoring the legislation.

The substantive provisions of the legislative reform proposal were a synthesis of the legal concepts identified and selected by members of the Ad Hoc Committee. The creative, original, and unique Wisconsin reform proposal based on community property principles was initially called "marital partnership property."

Drafting one comprehensive statute governing the property rights of spouses in dealing with each other and with third parties was a difficult and demanding task. The initial draft was introduced in 1979, with the expectation that feedback from qualified and interested reviewers would contribute to drafting a definitive and workable statute. The intensity of opposition of some "reviewers" did not prevent the bill's sponsors from continuing to seek all possible constructive suggestions.

Useful input came from: 1) groups concerned with third-party transactions with a married couple, such as financial institutions, realtors, insurance agents, retail credit associations; 2) representatives from the State Bar of Wisconsin; 3) groups of interested citizens. The input from these diverse elements guided each re-drafting of the proposal. This procedure was repeated many times because the intent of the major "architects" of the new property system (Professor June Weisberger and Representative Mary Lou Munts) was to develop a workable and acceptable legislative proposal.

Public Policy Education Programs

Several types of educational programs sponsored by different groups were launched to make the public aware of the nature of the public policy issue. The UW-Extension Womens Education Resources offered noncredit courses on the Educational Telephone Network with Constance ("Connie") Threinen in charge. "The Marriage Contract" was offered in 1974, and "The American Family: Legal Rx for Its Survival" was offered in 1976. The course covered historical analysis of economic and technological changes affecting the family and provided a comparison of community and separate property systems. The instructor for both courses was Linda Roberson, a Senior Legislative Attorney for the Wisconsin Legislative Reference Bureau.

The Governor's Commission, through its Executive Secretary Norma Briggs, prepared three distinctive publications. *That Old American Dream and the Reality or Why We Need Marital Property Reform*, published in 1977, was a slender 16-page brochure. It provided a brief exposition on: 1) the difference between a couple's traditional view of marriage and the state's view of the marriage relationship under existing Wisconsin law; 2) the origin of the separate property system including the legacy of Blackstone's interpretation of old English common law; 3) six case law decisions showing the inequities in the property rights of spouses. Three of these case histories were from Wisconsin and one each was from Nebraska, South Dakota, and Canada. This information pointed out that the public policy issue concerning spousal property rights was neither restricted nor limited to Wisconsin, but broad-based.

Real Women, Real Lives: Marriage, Divorce, Widowhood, published in 1978, was a 46-page paperback book. In-depth coverage of various aspects of the problems experienced by married women was based on provocative factual data from court decisions. The book was designed by Karen Foget, a graphic artist; Linda Roberson, an attorney who supplied many of the court case summaries; and Norma Briggs, the principal author.

The reader could identify with the problems and ask "What if this happened to me? Would I have financial assets, be entitled to pension benefits or Social Security benefits? Would I have to find a job and become self-supporting? What problems does a homemaker face in trying to re-enter the job market?"

The purpose of the book was explained:

> The writers of this book believe that all human beings—women and men—have a flourishing common sense and feel for what is fair. They want to move you to work together with them to make marriage an equal partnership and the family a stable place of refuge for us all.
>
> The idea of a book showing what happens to homemakers in real life first came in 1974. . . . It was then that the women of the state first made the Commission so acutely aware of the hazards of choosing homemaking as a career. . . . The Commission was overwhelmed by the chasm between the myth and the reality of the place of motherhood in American society. It determined to make the reality better known and more widely understood so that people could work toward bringing that reality closer to the dream we all share.[2]

The Marriage Partnership, published in 1979, was a 16-page bulletin. The first part presented 20 true-false statements. The answers explained the existing law applicable to each question. The latter part of the bulletin explained the provisions of the marital property reform proposal expected to be introduced in the legislature in 1979. The two-fold effect of the publication was: 1) to test the reader's knowledge of existing Wisconsin law and misconceptions about it; 2) to acquaint the reader with the merits of the marital property reform proposal.

The cumulative effect of these three educational materials was: 1) to provide authentic information in printed form that enabled a person to study and reflect upon it; 2) by inference to pose the question "Do you want to perpetuate the inequities in the property rights of spouses under existing Wisconsin law or do you think it is time to change the property system in Wisconsin?"

These unique educational materials were printed in quantity and available free for the asking. They were an important factor in educating people all across the state on the public policy issue.

In 1978, the League of Women Voters of Wisconsin published *His...Hers...Theirs: Marital Property*, a 36-page booklet. It was available to the public for a small fee. The Preface states:

> Marital property law is a highly complex subject. This publication is intended only to relate Wisconsin divorce, probate, and taxation laws to this state's marital property law. (The term "Marital Property" referred to existing separate property law.)[3]

"Marriage Wisconsin Style," a humorous and informative skit, depicted some of the problems encountered by married couples under the separate property system. The skit was based on case studies from *That Old American Dream and the Reality or Why We Need Marital Property Reform*, a publication of the Governor's Commission on the Status of Women. The skit was written by the Marital Property Study Committee of the La Crosse County League of Women Voters, and cost a small fee per copy.

These educational tools laid the groundwork for creating an awareness of the public policy issue embodied in the proposal to change the Wisconsin property law governing the rights of spouses during marriage and when that marriage ends with the death of a spouse.

Phase II: A Kaleidoscope of Events Associated with Wisconsin's Marital Property Reform

External and internal forces influenced the course of the comprehensive marital property legislative reform proposal between 1979, when Assembly Bill 1090 was introduced in the legislature and January 1, 1986, when the Wisconsin Marital Property Act became effective. Termination of the Governor's Commission on the Status of Women in 1979 prompted the formation of the Wisconsin Women's Network, a nongovernment grassroots advocacy organization. The public hearings on 1979 Assembly Bill 1090, on 1981 Assembly Bill 370, and 1983 Assembly Bill 200, held by the Assembly Judiciary Committee in the Assembly Chambers of the Capitol, revealed who supported and who opposed the bills. Lobbying by the State Bar was challenged and became a controversial issue. The media, daily and weekly newspaper reports, magazine articles, radio and television programs, kept the public informed about these different events and activities. To provide in-depth coverage of a particular event or activity, each is dealt with separately.

The Wisconsin Women's Network

The impetus for building the Wisconsin Women's Network came from an announcement by Governor Lee Dreyfus shortly after his inauguration that he would terminate the 15-year-old Governor's Commission on the Status of Women on June 30, 1979. This serious setback led to a regrouping which was of critical importance to the ultimate success of marital property reform. A grassroots advocacy effort succeeded the statewide, policy-oriented Commission which had launched the marital property reform.

On September 24, 1979, the formation of the Wisconsin Women's Network was officially announced with news conferences in about 20 cities across the state. The first issue of The Stateswoman, published by the Wisconsin Women's Network in September 1979, carried the story of the origin and purpose of the Wisconsin Women's Network:

> We endorse any effort that is made inside or outside of government to promote women's interest in Wisconsin, added Kathryn Clarenbach, one of the founding Network members and formerly chair of the Commission on the Status of Women.

"However, there has long been a need for independent power-
ful voices speaking out loudly and clearly on issues of concern
to women without fear of reprisal. The Wisconsin Women's
Network will meet that need."

The stated purpose of the Network is to create a network
of Wisconsin women and men to facilitate coordination,
provide a communications system and strengthen the advocacy voice for women's issues based on the principles articu-
lated in the publication *Wisconsin Women and the National Plan
of Action.* . . .

The founding organizations include: Wisconsin Women's
Political Caucus, Coalition of Labor Union Women, Wiscon-
sin National Organization for Women, Wisconsin Civil Liber-
ties Union, the League of Women Voters, the Center for Public
Representation, the American Association of University
Women, and many others [a total of 22].

Serving on the Network board of directors are many
prominent Wisconsin women including: Liesl Blockstein, Gene
Boyer, Kathryn Clarenbach, Catherine Conroy, Joan Dramm,
Eleanor Fitch, Nelia Olivencia, Vel Phillips, Chris Roerden, and
Louise Trubek.

Helen Casper, Madison, has been employed by the Network as the primary staff person.[4]

The internal structure, policies, and activities of the Network
were also described:

The Network will coordinate grassroots support for such issues as marital property reform, displaced homemakers,
ratification of the Equal Rights Amendment, battered wives,
women's health services, and affirmative action in employment.

The board of directors consists of representatives of the
subscribing organizations plus 10 members-at-large. The board
of directors will select the issues for Network action. Each participating organization will actively support only those issues
its membership endorses.

Marital property reform has been chosen as the first tar-
get for concentrated action. A task force, chaired by Anne
Arnesen, Madison, is being organized and coalitions are being
set up in each Senate district. A second task force on domestic
violence is chaired by Sandee Stone, Madison. . . .

The new coalition expects to keep close track of bills af-

fecting women and to monitor the voting record of legislators.

"The work of the Network is similar to what many existing activist organizations may be doing already on a separate
volunteer basis," said Gene Boyer, Beaver Dam, temporary chair
of the new group. "But we will bring coordination and
professionalism to the process."

It is important to emphasize that the Network is not intended to be another organization but rather a service to those
persons and existing organizations in our state who are
interested in seeing women develop some clout in the law-
making arenas.[5]

Comprehensive marital property reform was the top priority
issue of the Wisconsin Women's Network. The challenge was to
build immediately a coalition of advocates with political skills
who could persuade the legislators that the issue needed to be
resolved through appropriate legislation. On July 12, 1979, the
Marital Property Task Force was formed, with Anne Arneson as
the Coordinator. The article stated:

> The Task Force is setting up a coalition in each Senate district
> in the state. It has prepared guidelines to assist the coalitions
> and will provide continuing information, coordination, and
> encouragement. The coalitions will try to involve not only
> organizations which belong to the network, but also other con-
> cerned groups and individuals.
>
> The initial task of local coalitions will be to create public
> interest in the issue, to stimulate study and discussion, to edu-
> cate their community about the problem, to identify sources
> of both support and opposition in their community and to
> develop strategies to counter opposition.[6]

On October 15, 1979, a workshop on lobbying was held in
Madison. About 70 people attended. Many of the volunteers were
novices in the art of politicking. What to do, how to do it, and
when to do it were some of the topics covered by speakers
experienced in lobbying. A hand-out, "Some Do's and Don't's for
Lobbyists," taken from "Making an Issue of It: the Campaign
Handbook" published by the League of Women Voters of the

United States, was given to members of the group. "Successful Advocacy," a publication of the California Commission on the Status of Women, was called to the attention of the participants.

On October 25, 1979, the Coordinator sent a four-page letter to Area Coordinators and Task Force members. The letter covered lobbying, funding, literature, organization, and action. Volunteers were urged to start the process of contacting their legislators to encourage them to support the comprehensive marital property reform bill that would be introduced soon.

The letter urged groups to organize a public meeting in November or January with a panel discussion on the issue. The letter also included a report on the activities of a Coalition Coordinator, Judy Schwengel (Ozaukee Co.). It covered the groups participating, the committees formed, and the tasks assigned. The letter also reported the activities of Celia Lausted, a farm woman from Colfax who had been working on the marital property issue for a long time. Her activities demonstrated the importance of individual effort. Lausted was instrumental in getting a resolution supporting marital property reform passed by farm groups in the state.

> The following organizations passed Lausted's resolution or a similar one: Wis. Feeder Pig Marketing Cooperative; Wis. Pork Producers Association; Wis. Livestock Breeders Association; Wis. Extension Homemakers Council, Inc.; Wis. Farm Bureau; and Wis. Farmers Union.[7]

Volunteers were instructed to call or write their legislator as a member of the Marital Property Task Force of the Wisconsin Women's Network, not in the name of the Wisconsin Women's Network. This distinction was emphasized to comply with the policy of the Network: "Each participating organization would actively support only those issues its membership endorsed."[8] Hence, the Wisconsin Women's Network name could not be used to imply that the total membership, including all organizations, endorsed comprehensive marital property reform legislation.

The education of task force volunteers and coalition builders

was launched by providing essential information and constructive suggestions. The activities of the Marital Property Task Force
grew as it became more experienced in dealing with political
strategies. In 1982, questionnaires and candidate response forms
were sent to all incumbents and challengers in the September
primary and the November general election to determine their
position on marital property reform. The cooperation of the candidates was excellent, but the information obtained was useless
because all candidates stated they supported marital property
reform. However, who supported comprehensive marital property
reform and who did not remained unknown. As a result of this
experience, the coalition advocates subsequently identified the
comprehensive marital property legislation by name and number
of the bill to distinguish it from alternative reform bills proposed
by the opposition.

As the Marital Property Task Force became more aware of
the needs of local volunteers, a variety of services was provided.
Background material such as "Marital Property Revised: It's Still
the Way to Go" by attorneys Linda Balisle and Linda Roberson,
and "Answers to the Most Commonly Asked Questions About
Marital Property," by Professor June Weisberger, documents,
bills, amendments, memos, analyses prepared by the Wisconsin
Legislative Reference Bureau, prototype speeches, newspaper
articles, press releases, and Action Alerts (a request for immediate action to contact legislators), as well as press packets, were
distributed to the coalition leaders with the help of the Network staff.

The Madison Lobby Corps, composed primarily of Marital
Property Task Force members who lived in Madison, was very
active on a regular basis. The Madison Lobby Corps attended all
committee hearings of the Assembly and the Senate related to
marital property proposals. They attended weekly strategy meetings, developed strategy plans in conjunction with legislators,
organized a speakers bureau, and held press conferences. They
attended all sessions of the Assembly and the Senate when the
marital property legislation was debated and acted upon. In

addition, the Madison Lobby Corps was responsible for organizing receptions and functions, such as a breakfast or luncheon for new members of the legislature. Volunteers from outside of Madison came whenever there was a need to have a strong showing at the Capitol of people who supported the comprehensive marital property reform bill.

After the first coordinator, there were two co-chairs of the Marital Property Task Force. Zabelle Malkasian, Wauwatosa, and Jo Staab, Madison, were co-chairs for 1981-1982, followed by Mona Steele, Madison and Jo Staab from 1982-1990, when the Marital Property Task Force was terminated.

Helen Casper, the Wisconsin Women's Network Executive Director and Legislative Liaison, made marital property her highest priority during her entire period of service from the fall of 1979 through the summer of 1984. Her skill in keeping in touch with legislative developments on a day-to-day basis, in coordinating the task force activities, in supervising the educational programs, including the publication of *The Stateswoman*, and in managing the office was exceptional. Her leadership turned a fledgling grassroots organization into an effective, sophisticated political action group.

With the election of Anthony Earl as Governor in November 1982, the prospects for passage of the comprehensive marital property reform bill improved materially. The Governor and his wife, Sheila Earl, supported the bill. Roberta Gassman, the Governor's Aide on Women's Issues, was appointed the legislative liaison on marital property reform.

In 1983, Mona Steele was designated Chair of the Marital Property Task Force at the request of Jo Staab, who became the Assisting Co-Chair. This arrangement created a "command post" with all information received and dispersed centralized in one person with the Co-chair assisting. A coordinator for each of the 33 Senate districts was designated. Coordinators for each Assembly district were found by local volunteers. Also, a coordinator was designated in some cities. With this organization, volunteers could be reached quickly and networking was made effective.

With the incorporation of many of the provisions of the Uniform Marital Property Act into AB 200 in the fall of 1983, the momentum to pass the bill during the 1983-1984 legislative session increased. The efforts of the Task Force intensified, but optimism faded after the Republicans in the Assembly in effect destroyed the comprehensive marital property bill by amendments. Senator Hanaway's remarkable speech in the Senate on March 8, 1984 (reported on page 48), and the surprisingly large vote of approval for the bill in the Senate restored hope. The spirit of "Now or Never" took over. Phone banks were used to "rally the troops" of volunteers at the grassroots level to contact their legislator in the Assembly to urge a "yes" vote on the bill. Timing and coordination produced success. On March 13, 1984, the Assembly passed the comprehensive marital property reform bill.

Education Program

The Wisconsin Women's Network carried on an extensive education program concurrently with the development of volunteer grassroots lobbyists. The 1979 membership promotional brochure focused on marital property. On the front was a silhouette of a man talking to a silhouette of a woman. The message was: "When we got married ... we did not know." Inside there were silhouettes of men and women, and each made a statement that illustrated the inequities under the existing Wisconsin separate property law.

The Stateswoman, an eight-page newspaper published three to four times a year by the Network, was the primary educational tool used for keeping members informed on the progress of the reform proposal. Each revision of the legislative proposal was explained. Some members wrote articles on arguments in favor of comprehensive marital property reform, and others pointed out weaknesses of the alternative legislation offered by the opponents, particularly the State Bar. This flow of information began with the first issue of *The Stateswoman* in September 1979, and continued for the next six years. A Special Supplement to

The Stateswoman devoted entirely to the comprehensive marital property reform legislation was published in March 1983. It offered basic information on the need for and contents of the legislation. A subscription to *The Stateswoman* was included in the Network membership fee. Marian Thompson was editor of *The Stateswoman* from 1979 to 1982. Judy Taylor became editor in 1982.

The Marital Property Project, directed by Ingrid Rothe, was sponsored by the Network with UW-Extension, Women's Education Resources as co-sponsor. In the fall of 1980, conferences were held in Appleton, Eau Claire, Madison, Milwaukee, and Wausau. At the morning session, the keynote speaker addressed the question "What is Marital Property?" This was followed by a reactor panel consisting of legislators, homemakers, farmers, and attorneys who presented divergent perspectives on existing and proposed marital property systems. In the afternoon session, discussion groups focused on: 1) equal property rights; 2) the marriage contract; 3) taxes; 4) credit; 5) a spouse's right to will property.

The Network's education program did not stop with the signing of the Marital Property Act on April 4, 1984. The Wisconsin Women's Network was commissioned by the Wisconsin Women's Council, successor to the Governor's Commission on the Status of Women, in May 1984, to prepare ten "Fact Sheets."

The Wisconsin Women's Council was created by 1983 Wisconsin Act 27 to assess and improve the status of women in Wisconsin. It was preceded by a nonstatutory commission, the Governor's Commission on the Status of Women, which was created in 1964 and abolished in 1979. The Council is composed of the governor (or designee), six public members appointed by the governor, two public members appointed by the president of the Senate, two public members appointed by the speaker of the Assembly, two members of the Senate, and two members of the Assembly.

The "Fact Sheets" summarized: 1) the marital property agreement; 2) wills and estate planning; 3) bank accounts; 4) credit; 5) income tax; 6) joint tenancy and other forms of property ownership; 7) satisfaction of spousal obligations; 8) divorce. *The Wisconsin Marital Property Act Fact Sheets* were prepared by Jo Staab of the Network's Marital Property Task Force, with graphics by Karen Foget. These were published in May 1984, and made available for public distribution free of charge from the Wisconsin Women's Council.

In December 1985, the Fact Sheets were revised to include the 1985 amendments to the Marital Property Act enacted in the "Trailer Bill." The revised Fact Sheets were available for public distribution from the Wisconsin Women's Council and the Wisconsin Women's Network.

The December 1985 issue of *The Stateswoman* had a Special Supplement on the Marital Property Act. The basic provisions of the Act were explained. A series of questions and answers provided information on issues frequently raised by the public.

The Wisconsin Women's Network, in cooperation with the Center for Public Representation, published *A Marital Property Handbook: An Introduction to Wisconsin Marital Property System* in January 1986. It was prepared by Teresa Meuer, an attorney for the Center for Public Representation in collaboration with June Weisberger, Professor of Law, University of Wisconsin-Madison. The Handbook was designed for the lay person, and was available for a fee from the Center for Public Representation. (A second edition, which included the 1988 amendments to the Marital Property Act, was published in 1989.)

FINANCES

How were the activities of the Wisconsin Women's Network financed? Annual dues, contributions, and a few small fundraisers financed the Network's activities, with two exceptions. One, publication of *The Stateswoman* was funded by the Wisconsin Women's Education Fund, a non-profit, tax-deductible, public corporation dedicated to alleviating discrimination against women. The other, the Marital Property Project conferences, was funded primarily by a grant from the Wisconsin Humanities

Committee serving on behalf of the National Endowment for the Humanities.

The annual Network individual membership fee was $20, and the fee for organizations was $100. None of the money received as dues was used for capital expenditures. The office furniture and equipment were gifts or donations from Network members.

In November 1982, Helen Casper, the Network Executive Director and Legislative Liaison, reported:

> The Network does have a total budget of $34,000 and it is a fact that it costs $100 per day to coordinate advocacy on women's issues. . . .
>
> Contrast the $69,000 spent by the State Bar to defeat the Munts bill with our budget. (We thought we were big spenders when our postage budget on MPR [Marital Property Reform] exceeded $500 during the two months of legislative debate and action.)[9]

In the Annual Report of the Chair on June 23, 1983, Marian Thompson states:

> We continue to spend more than we take in, which means we must make extra efforts to raise money through fundraising events, through grants and personal contributions. Many members send extra amounts or tithe a certain amount each month. Others send in a check when they can. One person, very generously contributed $8000 to the Education Fund. The anonymous donor, who shared a one-time windfall, enabled the Network to hire Monica Wallace as administrative assistant while retaining Ingrid Rothe as a consultant.[10]

Fundraising events were few and widely scattered over the state. None produced much money—$200–$500. The primary source of funds other than membership fees was contributions made by members at the end of the year, or as a result of a phone canvas.

On January 3, 1985, Carol Palmer, Chair of the Network, made this report to the Executive Committee.

I was shocked to recently read that the Wisconsin Citizen's Utility Board has an annual budget of over $500,000! and the payroll for full-time employees is over $120,000.

In essence, the Network is a parallel organization—a state-wide advocacy group with a defined range of issues. Our budget is $34,000. And the Network's 'agenda' continues to be expanded as we realize all the many women's issues that demand attention.

Because we do not have financial resources that groups such as CUB have, our success depends on our volunteers, on 'follow through' and on dedicated services of our underpaid staff.[11]

The volunteers, who had the major responsibility for lobbying the legislators, paid their own out-of-pocket expenses. When they came to Madison to lobby members of the legislature, they stayed with friends or relatives. "In-kind" contributions made by the volunteers were particularly important. Sometimes it was services such as telephoning from home or typing at home. Other times it was contributing food prepared at home, as well as the time and labor needed for special events such as luncheon or breakfast for new members of the legislature. In June 1983, there were 400 members on the Marital Property Task Force out of a total of 1200 individual Network members.

There is no way to estimate the time spent or the value of various kinds of contributions made by volunteers at the local level in every part of the state. It is equally true that no estimate can be made of the time and out-of-pocket expenses paid by volunteers who came to Madison to use their political skills at the Capitol and those who lived in Madison. The Wisconsin Women's Network did not receive money from the state or the Wisconsin Women's Council. One can only conclude that the generosity of many people, women and men, and their commitment to resolve the inequities in the separate property system contributed significantly to the historic legislative achievement of getting the Wisconsin Marital Property Act passed by the legislature and signed by the Governor.

The Milwaukee Journal of March 14, 1984, had a front-page column headline that read "Volunteers helped push marital bill."

Much of the work that went into winning support for the bill (A-200) taking Wisconsin from a separate property to a shared property system for married couples was done backstage, however. It was done by scores of volunteers whose names never appeared on the program.

Mona Steele is one of those volunteers. . . . Steele estimated that she had devoted more than 50 hours a week to the project in the last month. . . .

Rep. Mary Lou Munts (D-Madison) Assembly author of A-200 said Steele and the other volunteers who had helped win support for the bill had been tremendously important.[12]

Governor Earl signed into law the Marital Property Act on April 4, 1984. A reception given by the Marital Property Task Force was held in the Assembly parlors following the signing ceremony. Here, friends and acquaintances made through volunteer work on the bill celebrated.

The Wisconsin Women's Network arranged a victory luncheon to cap the celebration. Helen Casper was the Mistress of Ceremonies. Four speakers highlighted different aspects of the drama that began in 1972. Norma Briggs spoke for the early pioneers and lawyers; Marian Thompson for the organizations; Mary Lou Munts for the legislative aspects; Mona Steele for the task force.

Assembly Judiciary Committee Hearing on 1979 Assembly Bill 1090

A public hearing on a bill introduced in the legislature is a normal part of the legislative process. The hearing provides an opportunity for the public to attend the meeting and hear the information presented by those who favor passage of the bill and those who oppose its passage. On January 15, 1980, the Assembly Judiciary Committee, James Rutkowski, Chairman, held a public hearing on 1979 Assembly Bill 1090, the first of the comprehensive marital property reform bills introduced in three consecutive legislative sessions. The hearing was held in the Assembly chambers of the State Capitol in Madison, and lasted from 10:00 a.m. until 7:00 p.m.

The Committee Record of those who attended the hearing was divided into these categories: 1) Appearances for and against the Bill; 2) Appearances for Information Only; 3) Registrations for and against the Bill; 4) Registrations for Information Only.[13]

Sixteen women and five men testified in favor of the Bill. The 16 women included Rep. Munts, author; 2 presenting Minority Reports of State Bar Committees; 6 representing four women's organizations; 7 representing themselves. The 5 men included Senator James Flynn, co-author; 3 representing organizations; and 1 representing himself—Richard W. Bartke, Professor of Law, Wayne State University, Detroit, Michigan.

One or more representatives of the following organizations registered for the Bill: American Association of University Women; American Milk Producers Association; Business and Professional Women; Coalition for Minority Women; Communication Workers of America, Local 5540; Division of Economic Assistance, Department of Health and Social Services; Fond du Lac Coalition for Marital Property Reform; Grant County Extension Homemakers; Langlade County Extension Homemakers; Lawyers Wives of Dane County; League of Women Voters from Beloit, Brookfield, Fond du Lac, Janesville, Marshfield, Waukesha, Wisconsin Rapids, Dane County, Door County, and Ozaukee County; Marathon County Farm Bureau; National Organization for Women from Door County, Madison, Sheboygan and Two-Rivers-Manitowac; Northport/Packer Neighborhood Coalition; Rape Crisis Center; Senior Citizens; Southwest Vocational and Technical Center; Wausau Mayor's Commission on the Status of Women; Women's International League for Peace and Freedom; Wisconsin Extension Homemakers; Wisconsin Women in the Arts; Wisconsin Women's Political Caucus from Dane County and Milwaukee.

One hundred sixty-six women and eleven men registered in

favor of the Bill. Of the 166 women, 117 represented themselves. These 166 women came from 50 Wisconsin cities, towns, and villages. They represented 49 communities outside of Madison distributed across the state. Nine of the 11 men represented themselves. These 11 men came from six Wisconsin cities, towns, and villages, with five outside of Madison.

Thirteen women and eleven men testified against the Bill. Of the 13 women, 3 represented two business and professional organizations; 2 represented the State Bar; 2 represented one women's organization; 2 represented one organization of men and women; 4 represented themselves. Of the 11 men who testified against the Bill, 7 represented the State Bar including the paid consultant, Richard W. Effland, Professor of Law, Arizona State, Tempe, Arizona; 2 represented one professional association; 1 was a legislator from the Assembly; 1 represented himself.

One or more representatives of the following organizations registered against the Bill: American Milk Producers Association Women; Chicago Title Insurance Association; Lincoln National Insurance Company; Madison Association of Life Underwriters; Massachusetts Mutual Life Insurance; Metropolitan Milwaukee Association of Commerce; New England Life Insurance; Pornography Group; Rock County Bar Association; Waukesha County Extension Homemakers; Wisconsin Association of Life Underwriters; Wisconsin Trustees Association.

Fifty-four men and forty women registered against the Bill. Of the 54 men, 42 represented themselves. The 54 men came from 18 Wisconsin cities, towns, and villages, with 17 outside of Madison. Of the 40 women, 36 represented themselves. The 40 women came from 17 Wisconsin cities, towns, and villages, with 16 outside of Madison.

According to the Committee Record, some women who were unable to attend the public hearing made their support for comprehensive marital property reform known by sending a petition to the Assembly Judiciary Committee. The petition sent by Josephine Muth had 103 signatures of Homemakers of Richland County in support of Assembly Bill 1090.

If gender, geographic dispersion, and organizations represented were indicators of who was interested in comprehensive
marital property reform, women from all across Wisconsin and
some men had a high level of interest in this public policy issue.
The challenge of these findings for the Marital Property Task Force
was to convert public interest into effective political action.

The Opposition

The opposition to comprehensive marital property reform legislation became more visible, more diversified, and more vocal in
each successive legislative session after introduction of 1979 Assembly Bill 1090. The opponents included the State Bar of Wisconsin, some business and professional organizations, some
women's organizations, and other groups. Their reasons for opposing comprehensive reform differed.

At the Assembly Judiciary Committee public hearing in the
Assembly Chambers on Assembly Bill 370 on June 8, 1981, and the
public hearing in the Assembly Chambers on Assembly Bill 200
on April 23, 1983, one or more representatives of the following
organizations either spoke against or registered against the
comprehensive marital property reform bills: the State Bar of
Wisconsin, the Wisconsin Installment Bankers Association, the
Wisconsin Mortgage Bankers Association, the Associated Milk
Producers, Inc., the Wisconsin Association of Life Underwriters,
the Independent Insurance Agents of Wisconsin, the Wisconsin
Land Title Association, the Wisconsin Realtors, the Wisconsin
Farm Bureau, the Wisconsin Institute of CPAs, and the Wisconsin Trustees Association. Women's organizations that opposed AB
370 and AB 200 were: Wisconsin Women in Agriculture, the
Wisconsin Farm Bureau Women, and Eagle Forum. One group,
identified later in this section, actively opposed all marital property
proposals, including the alternative proposals Assembly Bill 376
and Senate Bill 240.

The State Bar, as well as business and professional organizations
which appeared in opposition at the public hearings, based their

opposition primarily on the legal and economic impact of changing from a separate property system to a community property system. In addition to lobbying, the State Bar maintained a speakers bureau. Maryann Schacht, a Beaver Dam attorney and a member of the State Bar Marital Property Reform Committee, addressed the Juneau Chamber of Commerce on April 30, 1981. She said:

> Assembly Bill 1090—the Marital Property Partnership Reform Bill—is very frightening not only for lawyers, but the general public. . . . the 98-page bill is complex and not the kind of legislation that Wisconsin should have.[14]

The State Bar also carried on an active education program. In 1981, the State Bar published *Which Road to Marital Property Reform?*, a three-page brochure; and *Alternative Marital Property Reform Legislation Modifying the Common Law System*, a two-page flyer; and *Wisconsin Considers a Community Property System*, a 20-page bulletin prepared by Michael W. Wilcox. In 1984, *Wisconsin Considers Marital Property Reform*, a 20-page bulletin prepared by Michael W. Wilcox was published. All of these educational materials were published in quantity and free for the asking.

The Recommendations of the Governor's Task Force on Women's Initiatives were reported April 27, 1981, based on regular meetings the previous year. The Marital Economic Reform Task Force had been charged with:

> The responsibility of identifying the issues creating economic inequities in an on-going marriage. They were further charged with the responsibility of forwarding to the Governor recommendations for changes in policies, practices, procedures and legislation to rectify the inequities.[15]

The recommendations by the Marital Economic Reform Task Force dealt with support; procuring and use of credit; giving direction to investments; giving gifts; willing or passing property at death; taxes; and legal education about rights and obligations of spouses during marriage.

Marlene Cummings, the Governor's Advisor on Women's Initiatives, in her "Comments" states:

> There was the implication that to refuse to take a position in favor of adopting marital partnership property reform legislation was to somehow be against the attainment of equal partnership in marriage, to be against homemakers and to be against women as equal partners in family entrepreneurships (farming or small business). Not one task force member was against rectifying inequities.[16]

Initially, Wisconsin Women in Agriculture supported Marital Property Reform. In 1978, JoAnn Vogel, wife of a dairy farmer in Manitowoc County, Wisconsin, who was chairwoman of estate taxes for American Agri-Women and legislative chairwoman for Wisconsin Women in Agriculture, said, "We want our law to be more like the community property concept which recognizes that both spouses contribute to estate building."[17]

In 1978, one of the aims of Wisconsin Women in Agriculture was "to fight the widow's tax" both at the federal and state level.[18] JoAnn Vogel worked with legislators at the Congressional level to change the federal estate tax and at the state level to change the Wisconsin inheritance tax. In 1981, after Congress abolished federal taxes on interspousal transfers of property during life and at death, and in 1982, after Wisconsin eliminated taxes on interspousal transfers of property during life and at death, there was no evidence that Wisconsin Women in Agriculture supported comprehensive marital property reform. However, in the spring of 1983, JoAnn Vogel was one of four farm women who testified on the need for a model state—not federal—marital property law in Washington, D.C., at a hearing sponsored by the Drafting Committee of the Uniform Marital Property Act.[19] Why Wisconsin Women in Agriculture did not support the 1984 Marital Property Act, the Wisconsin version of the Uniform Marital Property Act, is unknown.

JoAnn Vogel addressed the Calumet County Farm School for Women in October 1985. A report of her speech states:

She identified the state's Marital Property Act, the first of its kind in the country, as something which will make "guinea pigs" of Wisconsin women when they have to pay attorneys in trying to get judges to interpret and apply the law.

The 68-page law, approved on April 4, 1984, and due to take effect on January 1, 1986, was passed very quickly through the efforts of a small group of women who were hurt by property settlements after a divorce.[20]

A December 29, 1985 newspaper article states:

JoAnn Vogel, President of Wisconsin Women for Agriculture, said her group had opposed a marital property law since it succeeded in getting taxes on interspousal transfers of property removed three years ago.

"We didn't need to have any more rights in our lives," said Vogel, a Cato farmer. . . . "We're too liberated already."[21]

After defeat of the Equal Rights Amendment to the United States Constitution, Phyllis Schafly shifted her attention to some of the economic problems of married women who fulfilled the traditional role of wife, mother, and full-time homemaker.

"Schafly Soldiers on Against the Feminists" was the title of an article in the February 28, 1983 issue of *Newsweek.* The article states:

Schlafly, 58, currently has her finger in a number of political pies. She is working for passage of state community property laws, an increase in income-tax exemptions for parents and a change in rules governing Individual Retirement Accounts.[22]

A copy of Schafly's proposal, "An Act to Provide Community Property Between Married Persons," was available for study in Madison in January 1983.

A contradiction between Schafly's actions as head of the national Eagle Forum and the activities of the Wisconsin Eagle Forum, appeared in Wisconsin in 1983. "Disadvantages of A-200—the Marital Property Reform Bill" was the title of a one-page printed sheet made available by Mary Dietrich, President of Eagle Forum—Wisconsin. Seven statements about AB 200 and the impact of a community property system were contained in the flyer. The conclusion states:

> These changes and any other that are truly necessary can be achieved by reforming our existing common law property system. It is not necessary to subject Wisconsin citizens to the chaos, expense and disruption that will result under a conversion to a community property system. . . . No other state is even considering such a conversion.[23]

A form letter on Wisconsin Eagle Forum letterhead dated May 28, 1985, and signed by Mary Dietrich, was sent to every member of the Wisconsin legislature. The letter urged the legislator "to support the one year delay on the effective date of the marital property reform law."[24]

Virginia Meves, who was the spokesperson for the Wisconsin Legislative and Research Committee at the public hearings on the comprehensive marital property reform bills, was also the Editor of the *Wisconsin Report*. It was published every Thursday by the Wisconsin Report Publishing Company, Inc., Brookfield, Wisconsin. The Education Editor was Erica Carle, and the staff was volunteers.

The January 10, 1980 issue of *Wisconsin Report* had a banner heading that stretched across pages 4 and 5 which read: "Hearing: 71 page Marital Property Reform Bill AB 1090." The article states:

> Do you remember how it all was in Germany as Hitler rose to power—the Health Plans for Children and Youth, the management of the people—the rules and regulations for all the people, etc.?. . . . Well, as one reads AB 1090, the Marital Property Reform Bill, it is as though the pages of History are being brought back and dumped on Americans, forcing Americans to suffer as the Germans suffered—economically too! Marriage is now to be reduced to a human experience— to be voided at any given moment if and when one of the partners so desires![25]

The September 22, 1983 issue of *Wisconsin Report* on page 4 had a heading in bold type "Marital Property Reform *Not*

Needed!" The article contained a petition prepared as a result of Seminars on the Marital Reform Bills. The petition states:

> We the undersigned are in opposition to the marital property reform bills AB 200/SB 105 and the alternative bills AB 376/SB 240 and request our elected state representatives and senators vote against *these* bills because: 1. They change the definition of marriage from a union (male and female) to a 'partnership of two equal persons.' (This could be homosexuals or lesbians and *no christian* can support this concept.) 2. They "abolish" or state "no rights to sexual and domestic services." 3. They allow "husbands and wives" (or "partners") to sue each other during marriage. 4. They bring in management and controls by agency, especially courts, lawyers, etc.[26]

In the same issue of *Wisconsin Report* (September 22, 1983) on page 8 the heading was "Urgent ... Urgent ... Urgent ... Help Defeat the Wisconsin Marital Property Reform Bills." A subheading was "Call, write, contact personally your State Representative and Senator *now* to vote *no* on AB 200, SB 105, AB 376, SB 240. The article states:

> Reform is not needed! Politicians are *obeying national commission on uniform laws* for creating new world government. No other state has adopted these radical changes for marriages/families. The family needs stability not change.
> All these bills are anti-God! All these bills are anti-religion. All these bills are anti-Christian and more! Wisconsin citizens stand now! Be faithful, loyal to God. Ask God's blessings on all who stand against forces of evil!
> Wisconsin citizens do not want forced equal rights—enslavement. Wisconsin citizens want individual freedoms: voice, choice.[27]

State Bar Lobbying Controversy

Lobbying legislators to try to influence their position on a bill under consideration in the legislature is an integral part of the political process. Some lobbyists are paid a fee for their services, either directly or indirectly by the organization or group they represent. Some lobbyists are volunteers. Generally, a paid lobbyist is skilled in the art of communicating with others, and knows what information is effective in persuading a legislator to support the position of the lobbyist on a particular piece of legislation.

The intense lobbying by the State Bar against the comprehensive marital property reform legislation during 1981 created a controversy among State Bar members, some of whom were strong advocates of the comprehensive marital property reform legislation. Four women attorneys took action and filed a complaint with the Committee to Review the State Bar, which had been appointed by the State Supreme Court. The 18-person Committee was composed of non-lawyers and lawyers.

An article, "State Bar lobbying protested," in the *Capital Times* for April 22, 1982, states:

> A $69,000 tab for State Bar of Wisconsin lobbying against marital property reform has some lawyers questioning how their Bar Association dues are spent.
>
> And some attorneys are raising the issue of whether the State Bar has any business getting involved in political issues at all.
>
> Four attorneys who share a practice in Madison have charged that the Bar's massive lobbying effort in the marital property issue 'far exceeded the permitted limits' for involvement in legislative activities.
>
> The attorneys, in a letter to the Supreme Court committee reviewing Bar activities, also criticized the Bar for never polling its members on the issue before taking a position.
>
> In fact, according to Jean Lawton, who wrote the letter with partners Anne Wadsack, Karen Julian and Karen Gast, the State Bar Board of Governors took a position against the marital property reform in December 1979, before any legislation was introduced. . . .
>
> The association spent $69,000 lobbying on the issue, including $8,000 to hire professor Richard Efflund of the Arizona State College of Law as an expert consultant. Ed Lien, lobbyist for the Bar Association, estimated that he spent 49 working days on the issue.
>
> The lobby funding comes from $70 annual dues of the

nearly 13,000 lawyers in Wisconsin, who are required to join the Bar Association.[28]

In the *Wisconsin State Journal* for April 18, 1982, a news item, "Hearing to address future of State Bar," states:

> Among matters to be considered by the committee are whether mandatory Bar membership should continue, the organization's internal structure, and delivery of services.
>
> Another subject for review is the Bar's controversial role in lobbying for pending legislation and supporting political candidates, activities that have drawn intense criticism from some members.
>
> As an arm of the Supreme Court, the Bar is a public agency and there are questions about whether such political activities are proper. . . .
>
> The group will make its recommendations about the Bar to the Supreme Court. . . .[29]

The Committee held a public hearing on the final day of the Bar Association's spring convention, April 23, 1982, in Madison. In the *Capital Times* on April 24, 1982, an article, "Wisconsin Bar practices raise lawyers' hackles," states:

> A number of attorneys questioned the legality of the Bar's active lobbying on legislative proposals. A recent $69,000 campaign to defeat a marital property reform bill came under heavy criticism as an 'unprecedented' partisan stand taken by the Bar without polling its membership.
>
> The issue was particularly galling to Rep. Mary Lou Munts, D-Madison, a Bar association member and sponsor of the marital property reform bill. . . .
>
> "Most organizations that lobby make sure their membership is unified on an issue before they do. If not, they're in trouble," Munts said.
>
> She called the Bar association's action on marital property reform 'rather shoddy and unprofessional' and said she was angry enough to resign from the Bar over the issue.
>
> Munts wasn't the only one who felt like quitting and her statement brought up what some Bar association members see as the fundamental question before the study committee:

Whether to continue mandatory Bar membership. Practicing lawyers in Wisconsin currently must belong to the Bar and pay annual dues, whether they like what the association is doing or not.[30]

The report of the Committee to Review the State Bar, which was sent to the Supreme Court, states:

The Committee . . . recommends that LAWPAC, the political action committee with which the state bar has been involved, directly or indirectly, in the past, be completely severed from the association. . . . The committee recommends that no state bar personnel or facilities be used in connection with LAWPAC, whether or not arrangements for compensation from the latter to the former exist. . . .

In the face of the committee's recommendations, we hold that, while lawyers may voluntarily form and participate in political action committees, it is impermissible for the state bar, funded as it is by compulsory member dues, to participate to any extent in LAWPAC or in its activities.[31]

In the *Wisconsin State Journal* for January 23, 1986, an article, "Forced support of State Bar lobbying struck down," written by Anita Clark, Courts reporter, states:

Wisconsin lawyers will no longer be forced to support lobbying activities of the State Bar of Wisconsin, the state Supreme Court ruled Wednesday.

. . . the Supreme Court said the Bar must establish an annual budget for legislative activities and determine each member's pro rata portion on dues bills beginning July 1.

Any member may deduct that amount from his annual payment, the court said. The total amount deducted will be subtracted from the lobbying budget. . . .

'The court concludes that the State Bar of Wisconsin should not use for activities intended to influence legislation any portion of the mandatory dues of those members objecting to such activities,' the Supreme Court said.[32]

The immediate effect of the complaint filed by the four women attorneys was statewide publicity of the division among lawyers, both men and women, on the merits of the comprehensive marital property reform legislation. The long-term effect on the State Bar was the 1986 Wisconsin Supreme Court policy statement governing the use of dues paid by its members. The repercussions of the 1981 controversy were still in evidence in 1988. The weaknesses of the Wisconsin lobby law were discussed in the April 1, 1988 issue of the newsletter, "Common Cause in Wisconsin." It states:

> It [the Wisconsin lobby law] allowed the state bar to issue an internal report showing $222,366 in 'expenses related to marital property,' while reporting only $3,600.[33]

The Media

Wisconsin media coverage of the marital property reform proposals over a six-year period contributed significantly to the general public's understanding of the issues involved. The media activities began at a modest pace after Assembly Bill 1090 was introduced in the legislature on December 5, 1979. They accelerated as the competing approaches to marital property reform intensified, and continued until January 1, 1986, when the Wisconsin Marital Property Act became effective. The newspapers (daily and weekly) magazines, radio stations, and television stations provided the information.

A list of newspaper articles that reflect the thinking of different people on the marital property reform issue is included below. The list is not exhaustive, rather it is intended to be exemplary of the range of subjects covered and the people who participated in the dialogue. Full information for identifying each article is given in Notes. For the present purpose of providing an "Overview" of the topics covered, only the title of the article, the date, and the name of the newspaper are given.

"Property reform called 'bill of decade,'" January 15, 1980, *The Capital Times*.[34] "Munts community property plan has opponents," January 16, 1980, *The Capital Times*.[35] "State must deal with property reform," November 30, 1980, *The Green Bay Press-*

Gazette.[36] "In most states marriage isn't a real economic partnership," December 2, 1980, *The Capital Times.*[37] "Equality begins at home: when it comes to liberation, homemakers just aren't making it," February 1, 1981, *The Milwaukee Journal.*[38] "Bills proposed to reform property system," June 9, 1981, *The Wisconsin State Journal.*[39]

"An even break: That's the goal of a new drive for marital reform," March 18, 1983, *The Milwaukee Journal.*[40] "2 West Bend lawyers push alternative to property bill," May 9, 1983, *The Milwaukee Journal.*[41] "Uniform marital property law needed," August 18, 1983, *The Capital Times.*[42] "Changes in state's marital property law would create chaos," October 1, 1983, *The Green Bay Press-Gazette.*[43] "Marital reform law will provide equal ownership," December 12, 1984, *The Janesville Gazette.*[44] "Marital Property Act: Equal split law a year away," December 13, 1984, *Greenfield Observer.*[45]

Although the Marital Property Act was signed into law on April 4, 1984, the 1985 "Trailer Bill," designed to facilitate a smooth transition from the separate property system to the marital property system, generated an intense political battle.

"New law forces move to Florida, Cudahy says," September 1, 1985, *The Milwaukee Journal.*[46] "Property law effects feared," September 10, 1985, *The Milwaukee Sentinel.*[47] "Don't be so quick to pan marital law," September 15, 1985, *The Milwaukee Journal.*[48] "Marriage partners in deed, too, Headaches await Jan. 1 startup of marital property law," September 22, 1985, *The Post-Crescent*, Appleton.[49] "Former foes unite behind 'trailer bill,'" September 22, 1985, *The Post Crescent*, Appleton.[50] "Marital Property reform act full of uncharted waters," October 1, 1985, *The Milwaukee Sentinel.*[51] "Why marital property law should be repealed," October 13, 1985, *The Racine Journal Times.*[52] "Marital law reflects partnership," October 13, 1985, *The Racine Journal Times.*[53] "Marital property reform seen benefiting all," October 14, 1985, *The Milwaukee Sentinel.*[54] "Brace yourself for a full-fledged fiasco," October 27, 1985, *The Milwaukee Journal.*[55] "Couples advised to prepare now for marital property law," November 5, 1985, *The Sheboygan Press.*[56]

"Property law not good for women, attorney tells Round Table group," November 15, 1985, *The Fond du Lac Reporter.*[57] "Complications expected on marital property law," November 16, 1985, *The Leader-Telegram*, Eau Claire.[58] "Some women don't like law," December 29, 1985, *The Milwaukee Journal.*[59] "Marital-law flap vastly overblown," January 5, 1986, *The Milwaukee Journal.*[60]

In addition to the articles listed above, the newspapers reported the progress, setbacks, and gridlocks encountered by the marital property reform proposals in legislative committees and assembly and senate floor debates for each of the three consecutive biennial sessions of the legislature.

A variety of magazines covered the marital property reform legislation. The *Farm Journal* carried two articles by Laura Lane. One was printed in the June/July 1978 magazine: "*Farm women, you have fewer property rights than you think.*"[61] The other was in the May 1983 issue, "Farm Couples ask: If marriage is a partnership why can't property be Ours?"[62] The Spring 1982 issue of *The Home Economics Journal* had an article by Karen Gobel, "Marital Property Reform: Wisconsin Home Economists Tackle Public Policy."[63] The January 1985 issue of *The Madison Magazine* had an article by Harva Hachten: "The New Marital Property Law."[64] The January/February 1986 issue of *AgVenture*, the Wisconsin Farm Bureau Federation magazine, had an article by Milton E. Neshek and Robert V. Conover, "What's yours is mine, what's mine is yours."[65]

Some radio stations had a series of commentaries on comprehensive marital property reform by opponents and proponents such as Mary Lou Munts' Reply to Frank Nikolay regarding Marital Property on the program "Morning People," WHA-Radio (Madison), July 2, 1979.[66] Also, Ed Hinshaw's "Editorial" on Marital Property Reform on WTMJ Radio, (Milwaukee), February 25, 1982.[67] Other types of radio programs included talk shows that encouraged listeners to call in and ask questions of the "guest-experts."

"Equal Partners: Wisconsin's New Marital Property Reform Law" was a television special presented November 13, 1985 on WHA-TV.[68] The program was designed to introduce Wisconsin citizens to the new community property system and to help them prepare for the changes that will have a far-reaching impact on virtually every married couple in the state.

The media coverage of the marital property reform legislation throughout the state provided a flow of information, factual, objective, and unbiased. This important educational service for the benefit of the general public contributed to an awareness and an understanding of the public policy issues involved.

Phase III: Legislative History of Reform Proposals

The comprehensive marital property legislative reform proposal was a focus of major attention in three consecutive biennial sessions of the Wisconsin legislature. Every step in the legislative process was used to promote enactment of the comprehensive marital property reform proposal and to attain its implementation. The legislative history of the proposal and its implementation is presented by legislative sessions.

1979-1980 Session of the Wisconsin Legislature

The "marital partnership property" proposal introduced as Assembly Bill 1090 in December 1979 had bipartisan support of 55 members of the Assembly and 14 Senators as co-sponsors. Representative Mary Lou Munts, (D-Madison), was its chief Assembly sponsor. The 1979 companion bill in the Senate was Senate Bill 474, and Senator James Flynn, (D-Milwaukee), was its Senate sponsor. At the public hearing held in the Assembly Chambers by the Assembly Judiciary Committee on January 15, 1980, Representative Munts explained the purpose of the proposal and invited interested parties to participate in its revisions and refinements. She explained the idea was to develop as nearly a perfect bill as possible through cooperative effort. The introduction of the bill created a storm of opposition from some members of the State Bar, and thus began the long haul of seeking detailed input from a very reluctant State Bar Special Marital Property Committee. The State Bar lobbying also was instrumental in destroying bipartisan support for the bill.

The bill was reviewed by the Judiciary Committee, and all the legislative committees which had an interest in any of its provisions. The bill did not include a provision for a state joint income tax return and for revised rates required to avoid major tax consequences if the "marital partnership property" proposal were adopted. The sponsors of AB 1090 recognized at the outset that the tax provision would require additional time to perfect, so no effort was made to advance AB 1090 beyond the Joint Finance Committee. Consequently, AB 1090 died in the Joint Finance Committee at the end of the 1980 legislative session.

1981–1982 Session of the Wisconsin Legislature

1981 Assembly Bill 370, a modified version of 1979 AB 1090, was introduced in the Assembly in the spring of 1981. Representative Munts continued as its Assembly sponsor. The 1981 companion bill in the Senate was Senate Bill 272, and Senator James Flynn continued as its Senate sponsor. The number of co-sponsors declined to 41 in the Assembly, and 12 in the Senate. All were Democrats with the exception of one, Representative June Jaronitzki (R-Iron River). The intensive lobbying by the State Bar had taken its toll. The lack of bipartisan support was to prove a serious handicap for AB 370.

The word "partnership" was dropped from the title of the proposal. One reason for the title change was "marital property" was the terminology adopted by the Drafting Committee for the Uniform Marital Property Act established in 1979 by the National Conference of Commissioners on Uniform State Laws. Subsequently, the title "Marital Property" Reform Proposal was used.

AB 370 included two tax provisions. The more significant one provided a state joint income tax return for married couples with a zero fiscal impact on state revenues. The technically complex provisions for changing from the combined individual state income tax returns for a married couple to a joint income tax return for a married couple that would be equitable and "tax neutral" were developed with particular assistance from Patricia Lipton, Director, Bureau of State Tax Policy, Wisconsin Department of Revenue. Assistance on tax policy was provided by Professor Charles Irish, Law School, University of Wisconsin-Madison. The other tax provision provided for the elimination of Wisconsin gift and inheritance taxes on interspousal transfers of property during life and at the death of a spouse. However, separate legislation to eliminate Wisconsin's gift and inheritance taxes on interspousal transfers during life and at death was subsequently enacted by the legislature in 1981 and signed by Governor Lee Dreyfus. The law became effective July 1, 1982.

In general, the opponents and the proponents of AB 370 agreed on the need to change the law governing the property rights of married persons, but disagreed on how to do it. The opponents of AB 370 believed that modifying the existing separate property system was sufficient. The proponents of AB 370 believed that it was essential to change the underlying philosophy and the basic legal principles on which the property system was based, if property equity for spouses in an ongoing marriage and at death was to be achieved.

1981 Assembly Bill 284 was introduced in the spring of 1981 by the opponents of AB 370. The 1981 companion bill in the Senate was Senate Bill 666. Changes in the existing separate property system proposed in AB 284 included the following provisions:

1) authorized a judicial partition of spousal property during marriage, using existing Wisconsin divorce law factors;

2) required creditors to extend unsecured credit up to $2,000 per creditor to a spouse not otherwise creditworthy based upon the creditworthiness of the other spouse. If a required notice

was sent by the creditors, the other spouse was liable for all debts incurred;

3) made both spouses equally liable for reasonable and necessary expenses;

4) increased the intestate share of a surviving spouse;

5) increased the surviving spouse's statutory elective share from one-third to one-half of the net probate estate;

6) authorized signed, written interspousal property agreements.[69]

Support for AB 370 and AB 284 tended to divide along political party lines, particularly in the Assembly, with the majority of the Democrats supporting AB 370 and the majority of Republicans supporting AB 284. Both bills died at the end of the 1981-1982 legislative session.

1983-1984 Session of the Wisconsin Legislature

1983 Assembly Bill 200, a revised version of 1981 Assembly Bill 370, was introduced in the Assembly in the spring of 1983. Representative Munts was its chief Assembly sponsor. The 1983 companion bill in the Senate was Senate Bill 105, and Senator Lynn Adelman, (D-New Berlin), became its Senate sponsor after Senator Flynn departed from the Senate. Assembly Bill 200 was co-sponsored by 41 members of the Assembly, and 12 members of the Senate. All were Democrats with one exception, Representative June Jaronitziki, (R-Iron River).

The opponents introduced a modified version of the 1981 Assembly Bill 284 in 1983 as Assembly Bill 376. The 1983 companion bill in the Senate was Senate Bill 240. Assembly Bill 376 included most of the provisions that were in 1981 AB 284 and added some new provisions:

The two main areas changed were credit and protections for spouses at death. As to credit, the $2000 limit per creditor was removed. Instead the liability of the nonapplicant spouse was limited to that spouse's Wisconsin gross income for the year prior to the one in which the debt was incurred. At death, where there was intestacy, the surviving spouse was given a choice between an increased intestate share and a property division using divorce law standards. The right to elect against the decedent's will was changed to a right to have a property division, using divorce law standards. Finally, a decedent spouse was given a right by will to direct his or her personal representative to initiate a post death property division action, using divorce law standards, if the will also designated beneficiaries for the property so awarded. This latter provision was drafted so that when the lesser propertied spouse died first, he or she would have a right to will a portion of the marital assets owned by the surviving spouse.[70]

These bills were never debated in the Assembly or the Senate, hence a vote on the bills was never taken.

The focus of the intense conflict between opponents and proponents of comprehensive marital property reform was Assembly Bill 200. The political posturing, obstacles, and uncertainties encountered during 1983 and 1984 kept this hotly contested legislation in the forefront of the news. To capture the spirited struggle between opposing forces, the suspense-filled days of March and April 1984 are covered in some detail.

In July 1983, the Uniform Marital Property Act (a draft of legislation governing the property rights of spouses during marriage and when that marriage ends with the death of a spouse) was adopted by the National Conference of Commissioners on Uniform State Laws. Peter Dykman, Deputy Chief of the Wisconsin Legislative Reference Bureau, was a member of the Uniform Marital Property Act Drafting Committee. (The Wisconsin Legislative Reference Bureau provides nonpartisan professional bill drafting services to the legislature.) The Uniform Marital Property Act offered both a challenge and an opportunity to the sponsors of AB 200. Should they propose a Wisconsin version of the Uniform Marital Property Act, or should they maintain their support for AB 200 (the comprehensive marital property reform bill that originated and was developed in Wisconsin)? There were strong arguments in favor of adopting a version of the Uniform Marital Property Act:

a. The philosophy, basic legal principles, and many of the substantive provisions in the Uniform Act were the same as those in AB 200.

b. The need for uniformity in the law governing the property rights of spouses was great. When there are significant differences among the states in this area of property law, the married couples most vulnerable to inequities are: 1) mobile couples, those who move from state to state during the course of their marriage; 2) married couples who own property in states other than the state in which they are domiciled.

c. In the area of commercial law a similar need for uniformity led to the widespread adoption by the states of the Uniform Commercial Code, the Uniform Partnership Act, the Uniform Securities Act, and other Uniform Acts.

d. Wisconsin had adopted a total of 46 acts developed by the Commissioners on Uniform Laws covering various areas of law. This was evidence that previous legislatures had recognized the benefits of uniform state laws.

e. Uniform definitions and uniform structure of the law contained in one comprehensive statute dealing with the property rights of spouses and with third parties would benefit currently married couples in Wisconsin and be advantageous in the future for all married couples when other states adopt the Uniform Act.

On the basis of these persuasive arguments the Assembly sponsors of comprehensive marital property reform introduced on September 27, 1983, Substitute Amendment 1 of AB 200, which incorporated most of the provisions of the Uniform Marital Property Act.

In the Assembly debate of Substitute Amendment 1 of AB 200 the opponents of comprehensive marital property reform successfully added a number of amendments to the bill. The most critical was the "opt-in" marital property system. The irony of this amendment was that it created an illusion. The amendment gave a married couple the right to create a marital property system if they took affirmative action. How a married couple could create an individual marital property system which would be judicially recognized as a community property system was a question left unanswered. The existing separate property system would remain the property law of Wisconsin. Unanswered was the question of how the complexities of two systems would be handled if both a separate property system and a marital property system existed side by side.

After the Republicans in the Assembly had, in effect, destroyed the comprehensive marital property reform bill by amendments to Assembly Substitute Amendment 1 of AB 200, adoption of a Wisconsin version of the Uniform Marital Property Act depended upon the action taken in the Senate.

Senator Donald Hanaway (R-DePere) and Senator Susan Engeleiter (R-Menominee Falls) strongly favored adoption of the Uniform Marital Property Act. They held a number of negotiating sessions with Representative Mary Lou Munts (D-Madison), Senator Lynn Adelman (D-Milwaukee), and Professor June Weisberger of the UW Law School. The result was the redrafting of a Wisconsin version of the Uniform Marital Property Act. On March 8, 1984, Senator Hanaway introduced AB 200, Senate Substitute Amendment 1. His 52-minute speech on the Senate floor was impressive, convincing, and effective in restoring bipartisan support for the comprehensive marital property reform proposal.

Excerpts from the Editorial Page of the *Capital Times*, March 12, 1984, convey the effect of Senator Hanaway's speech on everyone in the Senate chamber.

> State Sen. Donald Hanaway, R-DePere, rose to speak on the issue and legislation he had developed. . . . The Senate and the galleries quieted as Hanaway began.
> . . . Hanaway first spelled out the major effects of the bill without emotion, including the sharing of marital assets and the ability of each spouse to get credit on the income of both partners. The senators, reporters and lobbyists were actually listening.

Then he took the senators through the development of common law stretching back to Blackstone's writings in 1765 in England. The common law makes marriage paternalistic and takes a 'protective approach' to women rather than making them partners, he noted.

Hanaway quietly dissected his opposition before it could speak. 'Community property already is the trend in Wisconsin' he said, citing equal division of property at divorce and removal of gift and inheritance tax on interspousal transfers. . . .

Hanaway, himself a lawyer, was now closing in on his argument. 'The common law is out of sync with the way people are living.' Why, he wanted to know, should his two daughters be treated differently from his two sons when each marries?

He reminded his colleagues that this was 'not a Republican or Democratic issue; not a partisan issue; not a liberal, conservative or moderate issue. The issue, quite simply is: Do you believe marriage is an economic partnership? . . .'

The jaded troops in the press were moved. Reporters seldom file stories just on a debate or a speech, preferring instead to wait for a vote. On this day there would be some stories filed.

Prior to the debate, proponents took a head count and found 21 of the 32 senators ready to vote for the bill. Hanaway's masterful performance obviously pushed six more votes into the 'aye' column.[71]

[The Senate vote taken after the speech was 27 to 5 in favor of the Senate Amendment.]

On March 13, 1984, the Assembly took up AB 200, Senate Substitute Amendment 1. When debate on the bill began, the Republicans called for a caucus. Representatives Betty Jo Nelson (R-Shorewood) and Mary Panzer (R-West Bend) continued their opposition to comprehensive marital property reform. They made one more effort to derail the bill, and introduced 20 amendments. The amendment requiring creditors to notify the nonobligating spouse when the other spouse was seeking to obligate marital property was the only one of the 20 proposed amendments adopted by the Assembly. (The Senate concurred on this amendment later.)

The Assembly approved the bill by a vote of 59 to 38 on

March 13, 1984. Four Republicans, two men and two women, voted in favor of the bill. However, Lolita Schneiders (R-Menominee Falls), a member of the Wisconsin Women's Council, voted for the bill in order to qualify for the right of asking the Assembly to reconsider the bill.[72] This procedure was the last step in the legislative process in the Assembly, and it would give her an opportunity to vote against the bill. This last-ditch effort to "kill" the bill was unsuccessful. Several days later the move for reconsideration of the bill was rejected by the Assembly on a vote of 54 to 41.

Finally, the legislature had enacted a comprehensive marital property bill and it was time for advocates to celebrate.

On March 16, 1984, *The Milwaukee Journal* carried the story about June Jaronitzki and her lonely battle in support of the comprehensive marital property bill:

> Representative June Jaronitzki (R-Iron River) missed the champagne party, but shared the victory of passing a marital property bill. . . . Jaronitzki fought a lonely battle in the Assembly Republican caucus. . . . She was the only Republican [year after year] to vote for it [the comprehensive marital property reform bill]. . . .
>
> "So after the vote, I felt I had been a part of really accomplishing [one of] my personal goals [Jaronitzki said]. . . .
>
> "I made it very, very clear from the beginning that I was a strong advocate of a pure community property system. . . .
>
> "You have to give Sen. Hanaway the credit for saving the day," Jaronitzki said. "Everyone knows that Rep. Munts has worked very hard and diligently in the last six years on this and has laid the groundwork.
>
> "But what it really took was a bipartisan effort in the Senate to nudge a lot of people who were sitting on the fence."[73]

On April 4, 1984, Governor Anthony Earl signed the Marital Property Act into law. More than 300 people crowded into the Assembly Chambers for the bill signing ceremony. William Cantwell, Reporter for the Drafting Committee of the Uniform Marital Property Act, was a special guest. He congratulated Wisconsin on being the first state in the nation to pass a version of the Uniform Marital Property Act, and expressed the hope that other states would follow the example set by Wisconsin.

At the bill signing ceremony Governor Earl said:

> There are only a few moments in the life of a public official in which one feels one is participating in a historic moment of change. This is one of those moments, for me, and I know the feeling is shared [by] many in this room. . . .
>
> What we do here today will set a precedent of fairness and equity for the nation. . . . We are about to show the nation how to translate the sharing principle of marriage into legal and social reality. . . .
>
> This bill affirms marriage as an institution of equality and an institution of sharing. I believe it will strengthen family life in Wisconsin and add dignity to the marriage relationship.[74]

National and local television crews as well as national and local newspaper reporters were at the Capitol to cover this historic moment in legislative history.

The Marital Property Act repealed Chapter 766 of the Wisconsin Statutes entitled "Property Rights of Married Women" and recreated it to read Chapter 766 "Property Rights of Married Persons: Marital Property." The effective date was set for January 1, 1986. With this session the law became "fait accompli," and the major attention shifted to perfecting the law before implementation.

1985 Session of the Wisconsin Legislature

A "Trailer Bill" is a normal part of the Wisconsin legislative process when a new, comprehensive statute provides for major changes in the law. A "Trailer Bill" is primarily concerned with technicalities and practical issues of implementation of the enacted law.

The Legislative Council established a Special Committee on Marital Property Implementation on May 8, 1984. (A special committee submits its report, together with legislative proposals, to carry out their recommendations to the Legislative Council composed of 21 legislators. Proposals which are approved by a majority vote (11) are introduced as council-authored bills in the legislature.) The Special Committee on Marital Property Implementation was composed of three members of the Assembly, three members of the Senate, and three members who were not legislators. The Committee was directed to:

> Review 1983 Wisconsin Act 186, relating to establishing a system of marital property between husband and wife, to determine if, consistent with the Act's general intent, further clarification of the Act is necessary in order to insure a smooth transition to, and implementation of the marital property system. . . . [75]

On August 28, 1984, the Co-Chairpersons of the Special Committee appointed a Technical Review Subcommittee composed of the three Public Members: Professor June Weisberger, John E. Knight, and Michael W. Wilcox. The Technical Review Subcommittee was directed to review issues relating to the implementation of the Marital Property Act and to assist staff in refining draft language prior to consideration of drafts by the Special Committee. The Technical Review Subcommittee held 21 meetings between September 11, 1984, and February 14, 1985. This Subcommittee presented amendments to the Special Committee on Marital Property Implementation. Amendments on which there was a consensus in the Special Committee were presented to the Legislative Council.

The Special Committee on Marital Property Implementation met from July 1984, through March 1985. Questions submitted to the Legislative Council as well as those posed in articles and seminars were addressed. The recommendations of the Special Committee dealt with: 1) the integration of the Marital Property Act with tax, probate, and credit law; 2) clarifications of the original Act; 3) a few substantive changes not intended to alter the basic principles of the Act. On the basis of these recommendations, the "Trailer Bill" was drafted by Janice Baldwin, Senior Attorney, Legislative Council Staff; and Don Dyke, Senior Attorney, Legislative Council Staff who had done such diligent work on the bill throughout its passage through the legislature.

The original "Trailer Bill" was introduced as Senate Bill 150 on April 10, 1985, and passed by the Senate on May 7, 1985. It contained technical amendments that refined, clarified, and supplemented the 1984 Marital Property Act.

On May 21, 1985, the Assembly passed SB 150 with several amendments. One amendment would delay the effective date of the Marital Property Act for one full year, or until January 1, 1987. Another amendment would permit marital property agreements without any financial disclosure by the parties. These amendments were not acceptable to the Senate. On May 23, the Assembly voted to table the bill.

As a result of this impasse, the tax provisions of SB 150 were incorporated into the Biennial Budget Act passed on July 17 as 1985 Wisconsin Act 29. This action was necessary to implement the conversion from the combined state income tax returns to joint or separate state income tax returns for married persons.

Efforts to postpone the effective date of the Marital Property Act were vigorously pursued until the end of the legislative debate. Only when it became imminent and apparent that the Act would become effective January 1, 1986, with or without the "Trailer Bill," was the "court of last resort"—the Senate-Assembly Conference Committee—created. The Conference Committee was composed of three members of the Assembly and three members of the Senate.

Pressure was exerted on the Senate-Assembly Conference Committee to reach a compromise acceptable to both the Senate and the Assembly. Professionals (bankers, lawyers, accountants, merchants, creditors, real estate agents, etc.) particularly wanted the refinement and clarification of the Act as contained in the "Trailer Bill" to become effective on the same date as the Act, January 1, 1986.

The compromise reached in the Senate-Assembly Conference Committee made three substantive changes to the 1984 Marital Property Act (explained later).

The Senate-Assembly Conference Committee approved the substantive changes on a 5 to 1 vote. The negative vote was cast by the Assembly Minority Leader, Tommy Thompson (R-Elroy).[76] He held out for the delay in the implementation of the Marital

Property Act until January 1, 1987, and for his proposal to have two property systems (separate property and marital property) co-exist for five years on an experimental basis before a final decision was made.

The Conference Substitute Amendment to SB 150, the amended "Trailer Bill," was passed by the Assembly on October 11, 1985, on a vote of 73 to 24, and passed by the Senate on October 16, 1985, by a vote of 33 to 0. The Governor signed the "Trailer Bill" on October 22, 1985. Hence, both the amended "Trailer Bill" and the 1984 Marital Property Act became effective on January 1, 1986.

Late in the 1986 session Representative Richard "Dick" Matty, (R-Crivitz), introduced 1985 Assembly Bill 950 to rescind the marital property law. Again, in 1987, he made a similar effort to secure sponsors for LRB 1537 (Legislative Reference Bureau). No action was taken on either bill.[77]

1985 Amendments to the 1984 Marital Property Act

The amended "Trailer Bill" provided three amendments to the 1984 Marital Property Act. One amendment, sometimes called the "Wisconsin's Fruits" amendment, gave the owning spouse the right to unilaterally (without consent of the other spouse) reclassify the income or "fruits" (net rents, interest, dividends) of nonmarital property from marital property to individual property. To exercise this right, the owning spouse must execute a written statement declaring the "fruits" of his/her individual property reclassified as individual property, have the statement notarized, and notify the other spouse of the statement contents within five days after the statement is signed. Failure to give the other spouse the required notice of action taken by the owning spouse became an explicit breach of the "good faith" duty that spouses owe to one another in managing marital property.

Another amendment increased the "safe harbor" limit from $500 to $1,000 for gifts of marital property to a third person (one person or entity) per calendar year that one spouse may make without the consent of the other spouse. If one spouse makes an excessive number of gifts of marital property, even though each gift is within the "safe harbor" limit, such action may be a breach of the "good faith" duty to manage marital property that spouses owe to each other. This amendment did not affect the 1984 Marital Property Act provision that the amount of a unilateral gift could be larger if "reasonable" considering the economic circumstances of the spouses.

The third amendment had a limited duration. It allowed married couples extra time, if they so wanted, to adapt their particular situation to the new marital property system. This amendment provided for a statutory individual property classification agreement form for only one calendar year, 1986.

The statutory individual property classification agreement form was a "special" type of marital property agreement. A married couple (or a couple about to marry) could classify all their property (property already owned and property acquired during 1986) as the individual property of the owner by signing this statutory form of a marital property agreement. This "special" type of marital property agreement was enforceable without disclosure to the other spouse of each spouse's assets and obligations. It applied only during 1986 and automatically terminated on January 1, 1987, unless the spouses had terminated it earlier by signing a "regular" marital property agreement which required "reasonable under the circumstances" disclosure of assets and liabilities. A statutory individual property classification agreement could not affect either the support rights of a spouse or a child or the statutory rights of a spouse at death or divorce.

1988 Amendments to the 1984 Marital Property Act

The Special Committee on Marital Property Implementation, established in 1984 by the Legislative Council, was continued in 1986. The Committee studied the questions raised and the problems encountered in the implementation of the Marital Property Act. On the basis of the Committee findings, amendments to the Marital Property Act were recommended.

The basic principles of the Marital Property Act were not altered by the 1988 amendments that provided for: 1) expanded and refined definitions of domicile and of "held" as it applies to uncertificated securities and partnership interests; 2) authorization to reclassify a homestead and to reclassify property by a real estate deed signed by both spouses; 3) expanded management and control rights of the holding spouse of certain business property to direct in a will that the marital property interest and the "deferred" marital property election of the nonholding spouse in such property be satisfied from other property of equal value; 4) other technical clarifications.

The major substantive additions to the Act were the provisions creating two new statutory property classification agreement forms. One was the Statutory Terminable Marital Property Classification Agreement, a comprehensive agreement form that classifies all property presently owned by the parties and property acquired by them in the future as marital property. The other was the Statutory Terminable Individual Property Classification Agreement, an agreement form that classifies all marital property presently owned by the parties and property acquired by them in the future that would otherwise be marital property as the individual property of the owner. At the death of the owning spouse, property reclassified under this statutory property classification agreement is subject to special "elective" rights of the surviving spouse.

Requirements for a valid statutory property classification agreement common to both include: 1) the agreement form must be identical with the language set forth in the statute; 2) the duration of the agreement depends upon the financial disclosure of assets and liabilities (if no or insufficient financial disclosure is made, the agreement automatically terminates at the end of three years); 3) both spouses or a couple about to marry must sign the agreement; 4) the signature of each party must be authenticated by a Wisconsin lawyer or notarized by a Wisconsin notary public; 5) one spouse may unilaterally (without consent of the other spouse) terminate the agreement at any time.

1992 Amendments to the 1984 Marital Property Act

The Special Committee on Marital Property Implementation established in 1984 was continued in 1985–1986 and 1987–1988. At the request of Senator Lynn S. Adelman and Representative James Rutkowski, the Special Committee on Marital Property Implementation was established again on May 25, 1988. The Special Committee was directed to:

> ... (a) review issues relating to the operation and implementation of the marital property law to determine if further clarification and refinement of the law is necessary; and (b) examine where clarifications are needed in the relationship between the marital property law and the divorce laws.[78]

There were no amendments to the Marital Property Act in 1989 or 1990. Two bills based on recommendations of the Special Committee were introduced in the legislature. One dealt with the relationship between marital property law and divorce law and the confidentiality of tax returns of spouses and former spouses. The other bill dealt with clarifying the effect of marital property law on the amount and satisfaction of certain support obligations. Neither bill was enacted by the legislature.

Two amendments to the Marital Property Act were passed by the legislature in 1992. One provides for a number of minor revisions and clarifications to the Act. The other makes the surviving spouse's share of decedent spouse's deferred marital property under the intestacy rules automatic, rather than elective, when there are children of the decedent who are not also children of the surviving spouse.

1994 Amendment to the 1984 Marital Property Act

All the amendments to the Marital Property Act thus far have been Legislative Council authored, based on recommendations of the Special Committee on Marital Property Implementation, except the 1994 amendment.

The 1994 amendment to the Marital Property Act provides that if an employee "rolls over" all or part of a deferred employment benefit plan into an Individual Retirement Account (IRA), that (IRA) or portion of the IRA is subject to the special rules governing deferred employment benefits. Any other IRA or portion of an IRA not traceable to a deferred employment benefit plan is not classified as a deferred employment benefit. If the non-employee spouse precedeases the employee spouse, the marital property interest of the nonemployee spouse in the employee spouse's individual retirement account which is traceable to the rollover of funds from a deferred employment benefit plan terminates at the death of the nonemploye spouse.

1995 Amendments to the 1984 Marital Property Act

The 1995 amendments to the Marital Property Act contained in Section 7096 of 1995 Wisconsin Act 27, and in Sections 658 through 660 of 1995 Wisconsin Act 201, are nonsubstantive.

The 1995 amendment to the Marital Property Act contained in 1995 Wisconsin Act 418, pertains to divorce law.

1998 Amendments to the Probate Code that Affect the 1984 Marital Property Act

The 1998 Amendments to the Probate Code made extensive revisions to Chapter 861 of the Probate Code. A number of changes relate to the protections of the surviving spouse including the augmented "deferred" marital property estate "elective" share. These new substantive changes in the law governing the property rights of spouses in Wisconsin become effective January 1, 1999. They are explained in Part III.

The Wisconsin Marital Property Act enacted in 1984 was the forty-sixth draft of a comprehensive marital property reform proposal that was based on a rational and deliberate statement of public policy. The Wisconsin Marital Property Act probably is the most extensively researched and the most thoroughly drafted piece of legislation ever enacted by the Wisconsin legislature. The Special Committee on Legislative Implementation under the auspices of the Legislative Council facilitated the development of a high level of technical expertise, which guided the legislature in its subsequent efforts through four trailer bills during the next ten years to further perfect the legislation. While further legislative amendments may be enacted in the future, it is interesting to note that as the Act approaches the end of its first decade of implementation, there are no current legislative proposals for change, and little court litigation to date—January 1, 1999.

CHAPTER 2 🌿

History of Equal Rights Legislation

Overview

Legislation governing equal rights of women and men and property rights of married women have been linked together in the Wisconsin Statutes. In 1965, the state equal rights statute, originally enacted in 1921, became Chapter 246.15, a section of Chapter 246 in the Wisconsin Statutes entitled "Property Rights of Married Women."

Many people do not realize that there was a time in the United States when women did not have civil rights, and married women did not have property rights. *All* women, unmarried and married, were denied civil rights that were accorded to men, such as the right to vote, to serve on a jury, to run for public office, or to hold a government position. In states with a legal system based on English common law property rules, a woman lost her property rights when she married.

The movement to change the law governing the property rights of married women and the movement to secure civil rights for women began about the same time—in the middle of the 19th century. Each movement had a different focus and a different set of primary actors. State legislators, all men, initiated the change in property laws, and enacted the "Married Women's Property Acts." (See Chapter 4.) The legislators achieved their goal in a relatively short period of time, about 15 years, because property law is under the jurisdiction of the state. In contrast, the movement to secure civil rights for women was initiated by individuals and local nonprofit groups. Scattered, isolated efforts to change the law governing civil rights of women were limited in effect. Only when an organized national movement emerged that focused on one central issue—a woman's right to vote—was progress made. It took nearly 75 years of unrelenting effort to achieve woman suffrage.

The history of the woman's rights movement reveals that success on some issues at all levels of government was achieved, and that some issues remain unresolved.

Federal Equal Rights Legislation

The Nineteenth Amendment to the United States Constitution

The idea of equal civil rights for women was first expressed at the Seneca Falls Convention in 1848. Five well-educated women who felt the need for a public meeting to protest and discuss women's issues decided to call a convention. In her book, *Century of Struggle, the Woman's Rights Movement in the United States,* Eleanor Flexner provides the newspaper announcement that appeared in the *Seneca County Courier.*

> Woman's Rights Convention—A convention to discuss the social, civil and religious rights of woman will be held in the Wesleyan Chapel, Seneca Falls, New York, on Wednesday and Thursday, the 19th and 20 of July current; [1848] commencing at 10 a.m. . . .[1]

These women understood the requirements of a reform movement. They developed a Declaration of Principles using the Declaration of Independence as a model. In her book, *The Equal Rights Handbook,* Renne Tennenhaus Eisler says:

> To our Declaration of Independence, they added two words:

> We hold these truths to be self-evident: that all men *and women* are created equal.[2]

Thus, the equal rights declaration was formulated. To implement their Declaration of Principles, resolutions were prepared for discussion and action at the Convention.

Mrs. Elizabeth Cady Stanton prepared the final draft of the resolutions. Flexner reports:

> ... When she read her husband the draft of a resolution she prepared demanding the vote for women: Henry B. Stanton declared that if it were presented to the convention he would have nothing to do with the affair, and he would leave town. (He did.)[3]

Mrs. Stanton presented resolution nine to the Convention. It read:

> Resolved, that it is the duty of the women of this country to secure to themselves their sacred right to the elective franchise.[4]

Flexner states:

> This [resolution nine] was the only resolution not passed unanimously; it carried by a small margin.[5]

Because of the quality of leadership, the unique character of the meeting, and the development of an agenda, the Seneca Falls Convention is usually regarded as the beginning of the woman's rights movement in the United States.

The idea of a woman's right to vote was not only a new idea, it was a radical one. Public acceptance of the idea was slow to materialize. Between 1848 and 1865, Mrs. Stanton and Miss Susan B. Anthony gained the support of many others who shared their conviction that women had the same inherent right to vote as men. The total number of supporters was not large. However, it was encouraging and indicated that interest in woman suffrage was growing.

After the Civil War, the leaders of the woman's rights movement hoped that the issue of Negro suffrage and woman suffrage would be linked together. However, they were inexperienced in politics and unprepared for the kind of opposition they would encounter. To the politician the 2,000,000 emancipated male slaves in the South were potential voters, and the dominant political party was eager to increase the size of the electorate.

In 1866, the proposed Fourteenth Amendment to the United States Constitution was introduced in Congress. The second section of that proposal was designed to give newly freed men the right to vote, and it provided that right *only* for male citizens. Flexner says:

> Women with the acumen of Mrs. Stanton, Miss Anthony and Mrs. [Lucy] Stone were naturally appalled at the appearance, for the first time, of the word "male" in the Constitution. Its threefold use in the proposed Fourteenth Amendment, always in connection with the term "citizen," raised the issue of whether women were actually citizens of the United States. . . . Previously, the question of whether or not they (women) might vote had been regarded as a state matter, along with their property rights, marriage and divorce status, and legal position.[6]

The leaders of the woman's rights movement realized that if the proposed Fourteenth Amendment was adopted, another constitutional amendment would be required to give women the right to vote in federal elections. Mrs. Stanton and Miss Anthony were vehemently opposed to the Fourteenth Amendment unless the wording was changed.

Support for woman's rights by the American Equal Rights Association was generally acknowledged. However, the priorities of the Association were different from those the leaders of the woman's rights movement expected. Flexner says:

> The first signs of a split in the forces backing greater rights for women became apparent in the gatherings of the American Equal Rights Association, which was organized at the close of the war to further the interests of both Negroes and women, but whose emphasis under the leadership of Wendell Phillips, Horace Greeley, Gerrit Smith, and others shifted to passage of the Fourteenth Amendment at all costs.[7]

Six months after the Fourteenth Amendment to the Constitution was ratified in July, 1868, a Fifteenth Amendment was introduced in Congress which read:

> The right of the citizens of the United States to vote shall not be denied or abridged by the United States or by any state on account of race, color, or previous conditions of servitude.[8]

Mrs. Stanton and Miss Anthony urged Congress to include the word "sex" because it would be so easy to achieve both woman suffrage and Negro suffrage. However, in Congress the sentiment was strongly in favor of Negro suffrage and nonexistent for woman suffrage. With the ratification of the Fifteenth Amendment in 1870, universal male suffrage appeared to have been achieved in the United States.

A state referendum in Kansas in 1867 was the first political test of woman suffrage. The referendum was defeated. The state-by-state approach to the suffrage issue was time-consuming and the results unpredictable. In a few states women obtained partial or limited suffrage, such as the right to vote in presidential elections or in municipal elections, or to vote on school, tax, and bond issues. However, the permanence of these rights was uncertain. The legislation could be declared unconstitutional or rescinded by a future legislature. Women achieved the right to vote in the Territory of Wyoming in 1869, the first victory for woman suffrage. In 1890, Wyoming became the first state admitted to the Union with a constitution that provided for full woman suffrage.

The advocates of woman suffrage were women who wanted to participate in the public affairs of a nation with a republican form of government. They realized that in order to participate in policy making they needed political equality with men. The opponents of woman suffrage believed women were not qualified to be a part of the turmoil and battle of public life, and that women should not be in an adversary position with men. They believed woman suffrage would destroy women's femininity.

In May 1869, Mrs. Stanton called for a woman suffrage amendment to the Constitution at the annual meeting of the American

Equal Rights Association. This issue split the Association into two factions. Immediately after the meeting Mrs. Stanton and Miss Anthony organized the National Woman Suffrage Association. Membership was limited to women only. Flexner says:

> They did so in the belief that it was largely due to the preponderance of men in the Equal Rights Association leadership that women's interests had been betrayed, and that women who followed the men's lead—Mrs. Stone, Mrs. [Julia Ward] Howe, and others—had been misled or duped by them.[9]

A second organization, calling itself the American Woman Suffrage Association, was established in November 1869. As late as 1896, the American Woman Suffrage Association" (although paying lip service to a federal amendment) turned its energies to amending the constitutions of the individual states."[10]

This split in the woman's movement was detrimental to the suffrage movement. The two organizations had the same basic aims, but it was their "deeply opposing social viewpoints—the conservative and the radical—which clashed, not on whether women should vote, but on *how* that goal could be won."[11] The two suffrage associations operated independently for twenty years. Reconciliation and merger brought some progress, but the issue of state versus federal action was not resolved. Between 1870 and 1910, the success of the "alternative route" of amending state constitutions to provide woman suffrage was neither impressive nor promising in its achievements.

In 1878, a woman suffrage amendment, usually referred to as the "Anthony Amendment," was introduced in Congress. It read: "The right of citizens of the United States to vote shall not be denied or abridged by the United States or by any state on account of sex."[12] This wording remained unchanged until the amendment was finally passed by Congress in 1919.

After 1893, the federal woman suffrage amendment practically disappeared as a political issue until it was revived in 1913. The federal amendment was defeated in the Senate in 1914 and in the House of Representatives in 1915.

The advocates of the federal amendment understood that political action and cooperation of diverse elements at every level of government were required. World War I brought women out of their homes, and they concentrated their efforts on performing their patriotic duty in a time of national crisis. As Flexner reports:

> Like the Civil War, World War I brought women out of their homes into new spheres of action, and thousands more into work no longer new to them. The enormous influx of women into industrial work and public service sharply altered their standing in the community. It also furnished them with a new, heightened argument: if democracy began at home, surely the most immediate application must be to those who were shouldering, and competently discharging, every kind of social responsibility, and by so doing, proving once and for all their competence to assume political responsibility as well.[13]

The federal woman suffrage amendment was passed by the House of Representatives on January 10, 1918, and reenacted on May 20, 1919. But it took the election of a new Congress and the defeat of two senators who opposed woman suffrage to get Senate passage of the amendment on June 4, 1919.

On June 10, 1919, Wisconsin became the first state in the nation to ratify the Nineteenth Amendment to the United States Constitution giving women the right to vote. This historic achievement was not an accident. In her book, *On Wisconsin Women*, Genevieve McBride describes how it happened. She states:

> In Wisconsin, wrote [Mrs. Theodora] Youmans, "our lobby got settled to its task"; as women anticipated every detail down to legal language of ratification and a recommendation to the governor of a courier to carry the document to Washington: David G. James, seventy-six years old and retired from the legislature where he had sponsored the 1912 referendum bill but in Madison for the day.
>
> In Wisconsin, women divided by differences over strategies and tactics worked together again to win the ratification race: with Youmans in the Capitol was Ada James, whose "traveling bag" was "commandeered" by her father. By train, by car,

and on foot, he went to Washington, D.C. There, women had alerted Wisconsin Senator Irvine L. Lenroot, a longtime suffragist who awaited James's arrival and expedited the document to the State Department—and then telegraphed confirmation to Youmans.

For weeks women waited for further word from Washington, until the secretary of state sent Youmans official verification: on June 10, 1919, Wisconsin at last earned its place in suffrage history.[14]

Fourteen months later, on August 26, 1920, Tennessee became the 36th state to ratify the Nineteenth Amendment to the United States Constitution, and ratification by the necessary three-fourths of the state legislatures was finally achieved.

In contrast to the 75 years it took to change the law on voting, the law governing the property rights of women in the United States changed in a relatively short period of time, 1848 to 1863. Thurman in her study of the Married Women's Property Acts concludes:

> . . . the acts were adopted with a speed suggesting that they responded to and embodied ideas of women's roles and just business expectations that were already well established in social attitudes and behavior. As a marked contrast to the women's suffrage drive, the development of the Married Women's Property Acts apparently represents a case where legal processes ratified rather than helped generate social change.[15]

In contrast with the Married Women's Property Acts, which were passed voluntarily and independently by states, the proposed 19th Amendment to the United States Constitution would be a federal mandate to give all women the right to vote in all elections in every state. This would result in a radical change in the traditional political process. The woman suffrage drive could even be viewed as a challenge "to the *state*—an all-male government."[16] Hence, many years of hard work and dedication by women and men who believed in political equality were required to achieve social change of this magnitude. It took nearly 75 years of effort to generate a favorable attitude toward woman suffrage and public acceptance of the 19th Amendment to the United States Constitution giving women the right to vote.

THE PROPOSED EQUAL RIGHTS AMENDMENT
TO THE UNITED STATES CONSTITUTION

The Equal Rights Amendment to the United States Constitution approved by Congress in 1972 was the second effort to establish full-fledged constitutional equality of women and men. From their experience in achieving suffrage the leaders of the woman's rights movement believed that a permanent right of equality for women could be achieved only by a comprehensive or overall amendment to the United States Constitution. Alice Paul, of the National Women's Party, wrote the Equal Rights Amendment that was introduced in Congress in 1923.

Excerpts from a League of Women Voters publication show that Alice Paul's perception of the importance of an Equal Rights Amendment was not shared initially by the general public.

> It [the amendment] received little support from women's organizations such as the League, the American Association of University Women, the National Federation of Business and Professional Women's Clubs, the National Consumers' League and the National Women's Trade Union League.... The League of Women Voters actively opposed the amendment in the 1920s fearing it was too radical and would endanger hard-won protective legislation for women.... In 1937, the National Federation of Business and Professional Women's Clubs was the first major organization to break the freeze and endorse the amendment.... The League supported the step-by-step approach to equality of rights throughout the 1940s.[17]

In 1954, the League dropped its opposition to the Equal Rights Amendment. In May 1972, at the League's national convention the delegates voted overwhelmingly to support the ERA.

> With this decisive action the League, as the lineal descendant of the original women's movement, came full circle to give priority support to equal rights for men and women.[18]

The Equal Rights Amendment had a long history in Congress from its introduction in 1923, its reintroduction in each successive Congress, to its passage by Congress in 1972. The first version of the Equal Rights Amendment was "Men and women shall have equal rights throughout the United States and every place subject to its jurisdiction."[19] In 1943, the wording was changed to "Equality of rights under the law shall not be denied or abridged by the United States or by any State on account of sex."[20]

As a political issue in Congress, the Equal Rights Amendment was not viewed as a significant issue until gender or sex based discrimination became a matter of public debate. The woman's rights movement was rekindled by the civil rights movement in the 1960s. The parallels between the status of women and that of minorities became an energizing force for women's organizations. The public debate was reinforced in 1971 by the United States Supreme Court decision that a State law explicitly favoring men as administrators of intestate estates was invalid.[21] It was the first time the Supreme Court had ruled that gender or sex based discrimination was unconstitutional.

The Senate Judiciary Committee reported favorably on the Equal Rights Amendment in eight different Congresses. Twice the Senate, in the 81st and 83rd Congresses, passed the resolution with a floor amendment, but the House of Representatives did not act on the measure. The Senate floor amendment, known as the Hayden amendment, read that the amendment "shall not be construed to impair any rights, benefits, or exemptions now or hereafter conferred by law upon members of the female sex."[22] This amendment diluted the goal of the Equal Rights Amendment which was equality under the law, hence the advocates of an Equal Rights Amendment rejected the Hayden amendment.

On August 10, 1970, the House of Representatives passed the Equal Rights Amendment unamended. However, the Senate added amendments that were unacceptable to the House.

In the new Congress of 1971, both the Senate and the House Judiciary Committees held extensive hearings on the Equal Rights Amendment. There was full debate in the Senate and the House. Committee reports explaining the amendment were issued. As a result the "legislative history" of the Equal Rights Amendment, the source the United States Supreme Court looks to in interpreting an amendment, was firmly established. Pressure by women's organizations led by Congresswoman Martha Griffiths resulted in action by Congress. On October 12, 1971, the House of Representatives voted 354 to 23 in favor of the amendment. On March 22, 1972, the Senate voted 84 to 8 to approve the amendment.

The Equal Rights Amendment passed by Congress read:

Section 1. Equality of rights under the law shall not be denied or abridged by the United States or by any State on account of sex.
Section 2. The Congress shall have the power to enforce, by appropriate legislation, the provisions of this article.
Section 3. This amendment shall take effect two years after the date of ratification.[23]

Ratification of the amendment began with great enthusiasm. Wisconsin ratified the amendment on April 20, 1972. By the end of 1975, 34 of the needed 38 states had ratified the amendment. A survey of the adult population in the continental United States made by Roper Research, Inc. in 1975, showed that 61% favored the amendment; 20% opposed; and 19% had mixed feelings.[24] With these favorable signs pointing to early ratification by three-fourths of the states (38 out of 50), the advocates for the ERA were taken by surprise when ratification came to a halt in 1976.

ERAmerica, an umbrella organization composed of more than 100 organizations advocating the ERA, was formed in February 1976. The purpose was to unify programs and resources and coordinate the expertise and talent available. The newly created ERAmerica assumed the leadership role in the campaign to get state ratification of the amendment. In targeted states a coordinated, aggressive lobbying effort of state legislators was undertaken. Grassroot groups and campaigns to elect state legislators who supported the amendment were organized. As a safety measure Congress was asked to extend the time period for ratification in case the original seven-year period proved insufficient. Congress passed a resolution extending the ratification deadline for three years, from March 22, 1979, to June 30, 1982. The struggle for ratification in targeted states intensified and continued unabated until June 30, 1982.

Organized opposition to the ERA first surfaced in 1973. Through misinformation on the meaning and impact of the amendment, misconceptions and unfounded folklore designed to play on the fears of people were generated, such as men and women would have to use the same public restrooms. These strategies worked, and the opponents defeated ratification of the amendment in several states. STOP-ERA worked to rescind ratification in states that had previously voted in favor of ratification, and were successful in Nebraska and Tennessee. Although the legal standing of recision was unknown, the idea had an enormous psychological effect on people who were trying to reach a personal decision on the merits of the ERA. It was a pitched battle between advocates and opponents to the bitter end. On June 30, 1982, only 35 states had ratified the amendment, three short of the 38 needed to make the amendment part of the U.S. Constitution. Hence, the Equal Rights Amendment went down in defeat.

The opponents of the ERA were ecstatic over their victory. "Schlafly celebrates defeat of ERA" was a heading in *The Capital Times* for July 1, 1982. The article states:

> Schlafly, the amendment's most prominent foe, was hailed as a constitutional heroine at a banquet Wednesday night, just before the midnight deadline for ratification expired.
>
> Generals, senators, clerics, commentators, legislators and lawyers saluted her 10-year fight to prevent ratification. . . .
>
> Schlafly, a mother of six from Alton, Ill., has been more closely identified with the opposition to the ERA than anyone else. Her organization, Eagle Forum, sponsored the Shoreham ballroom celebration dinner.
>
> She was hailed by Interior Secretary James Watt, Gen. Daniel Graham, Sens. [Jesse] Helms, [R-NC] and Jeremiah Denton, R-Ala., Brig. Gen. Andrew Gatsis, the Rev. Jerry Falwell, media critic Reed Irvin, conservative strategist Paul Weyrich and many others.

Presidential aide Morton Blackwell presented her with a 425-carat ruby the size of a coffee cup saucer and the same color and shape as her red eight-sided "Stop ERA" buttons.[25]

Lack of success in 1982 in securing ratification of the ERA in three-fourths of the states did not mean the issue was dead or abandoned. On the contrary, the proponents recognized a different strategy was necessary. The consensus among advocates for the amendment was that a more effective strategy to insure ratification at the state level must be in place and ready to function if and when Congress again passes an Equal Rights Amendment.

CONSTITUTIONAL EQUALITY OF WOMEN AND MEN

Constitutional equality was expressed in the Declaration of Independence as a basic principle of a republican form of government. The significance of constitutional equality was first recognized by the women who convened the Seneca Falls Convention in 1848.

The Declaration of Independence contains two revolutionary ideas: 1) governments derive their power "from the consent of the governed"; 2) "all men are created equal." These two revolutionary ideas were identified, and their importance to American women in the 20th century was underscored by William B. Aycock, Kenan Professor of Law, University of North Carolina, in a 1975 address to a meeting sponsored by the National Committee on the Observance of International Women's Year.[26]

Aycock noted that the 19th Amendment to the United States Constitution turned the first revolutionary idea into reality for American women. The 19th Amendment established a woman's right to vote and to be an active participant in a republican form of government. Today, the number of women who participate in the political process and who are elected to public office at the federal, state, and local levels of government is substantial. Their role in public policy making and in decision making at all levels of government means that women are now an integral part of the governments that derive their power "from the consent of the governed." The first federal legislation adopted in the United States that incorporated the idea of all women as full-fledged constitutional equals of men was the 19th Amendment to the United States Constitution.

Supporters of an Equal Rights Amendment to the United States Constitution continue to believe that such an amendment is necessary to transform the second revolutionary idea into reality for American women. It would require the federal government and all state and local governments to treat each person, male and female, as an individual human being without regard to gender. Legal equality would require the language of the laws to be gender neutral. An Equal Rights Amendment would prohibit discrimination against men on the basis of gender, as well as against women. The amendment would apply only to government action at the federal, state, or local level. However, Title VII of the Civil Rights Act of 1964, which prohibited discrimination in employment on the basis of race, religion, sex, and national origin, would continue to apply in the private sector of the nation. The ERA would not affect purely private or social actions that may be discriminatory. How long it will take the nation to adopt a constitutional change that explicitly embodies the idea of all women as full-fledged equals of men in an Equal Rights Amendment to the United States Constitution is unknown.

Wisconsin Equal Rights Legislation

The Wisconsin equal rights statute passed in 1921 was the first law in the nation enacted by a state legislature to eliminate almost all legal discriminations against women. Hence, Chapter 529, Laws of 1921—"An Act to create new section 6.015 of the statutes to remove discriminations against women and to give them equal rights before the law"—is a historic piece of legislation. The statute reads:

Section 1. A new section is added to the statutes to read: 6.015 Women shall have the same rights and privileges under the law as men in the exercise of suffrage, freedom of contract, choice of residence for voting purposes, jury service, holding office, holding and conveying property, care and custody of children, and in all other respects. The various courts, executive and administrative officers shall construe the statutes where masculine gender is used to include the feminine gender unless such construction will deny to females the special protection and privileges which they now enjoy for the general welfare. The courts, executive and administrative officers shall make all necessary rules and provisions to carry out the intent and purpose of this statute.

Section 2. Any woman drawn to serve as a juror upon her request to the presiding judge or magistrate, before the commencement of the trial or hearing, shall be excused from the panel or venire.

Section 3. This act shall take effect upon passage and publication.[27]

(Approved July 11, 1921. Published July 15, 1921)

In the 1965 Wisconsin Statutes, the equal rights statute was incorporated as section 246.15 of Chapter 246 entitled "Property Rights of Married Women." The equal rights statute was virtually unchanged from its enactment in 1921, until amended by the Wisconsin 1975 "omnibus bill."

An Equal Rights Amendment to the Wisconsin Constitution was passed by the state legislature in two consecutive sessions— 1971 and 1973. The proponents of the Amendment considered approval of it in a statewide referendum as almost certain. However, on April 3, 1973, the voters unexpectedly rejected the Equal Rights Amendment (1973 Enrolled Joint Resolution 5) to the Wisconsin Constitution by a vote of 447,240 to 520,936.[28]

Representative Marjorie "Midge" Miller, (D-Madison) Chair of the Assembly Equal Rights Committee, authored the Wisconsin resolution to ratify the Equal Rights Amendment to the United States Constitution. It was passed by Congress on March 22, 1972 and ratified on April 20, 1972, in a special session of the state legislature. Wisconsin was the fifteenth state to ratify the ERA. The legislature anticipated speedy ratification of the ERA by the necessary three-fourths of the states and that the ERA would become the law of the land in just a few years.

The process of reviewing the Wisconsin statutes to implement the anticipated ERA was initiated by the legislature in 1972. A Special Committee of the Legislative Council was directed to study those state statutes that differentiated on the basis of sex and to recommend changes that would provide equal protection under the law for both women and men.

The February 23, 1973, Legislative Council Report to the 1973 Legislature on Equal Rights identified 280 statutory provisions that treated men and women differently. To remedy these inequities a comprehensive bill (referred to as an "omnibus bill" because it consists of a number of miscellaneous provisions) was needed.

1973 Assembly Bill 23, the "omnibus bill," authored by Representative Miller, mandated the removal of sexually discriminatory language from the state statutes. The Assembly passed AB 23 in 1973 but the Senate failed to pass it when its most vocal opponent, Senator Gordon Roseleip, (R-Platteville), held the bill in committee on the basis that the electorate had failed to approve the Equal Rights Amendment to the Wisconsin Constitution.

1975 Assembly Bill 431, a revised version of the 1973 Assembly Bill 23, authored by Representative Miller, mandated the removal of sexually discriminatory language from the state statues in all areas of law except sexual assault, divorce and property rights of spouses during marriage. These areas of law were excluded because the sponsors of the "omnibus bill" believed there was a need to examine more thoroughly the basic principles in each of these areas of law before reform proposals could be developed. 1975 Assembly Bill 431 was passed by the Wisconsin legislature on September 26, 1975.[29] Chapter 94, Laws of 1975—"An Act . . . relating to eliminating from the statutes distinctions between persons based on sex"—contains the provisions of the "omnibus bill."[30] It is sometimes called the 1975 Wisconsin Equal Rights Act.

The "omnibus bill" changed the language of the equal rights provision of Chapter 246 "Property Rights of Married Women" Section 246.15 (1975 Wisconsin Statutes) to read:

> *Equal rights.* Women and men shall have the same rights and privileges under law in the exercise of suffrage, freedom of contract, choice of residence for voting purposes, jury service, holding office, holding and conveying property, care and custody of children, and in all other respects. The various courts, executive and administrative officers shall construe the statutes so that words importing one gender extend and may be applied to any gender consistent with the manifest intent of the legislature. The courts, executive and administrative officials shall make all necessary rules and provisions to carry out the intent and purpose of this section.[31]

The equal rights provision of the 1984 Marital Property Act remained the same as it was in the 1981 Wisconsin Statutes (Section 766.15), except for the deletion of three words "for voting purposes" in connection with the choice of residence. However, the equal rights provision in the 1984 Marital Property Act was changed from a section to a subsection, and renumbered 766.97(1) Equal Rights, and the subsection was expanded to include 766.97(2) and 766.97(3) which abolished all remaining English common law disabilities of married women.[32]

The three areas of law excluded from the 1975 "omnibus bill" were dealt with subsequently. A landmark piece of legislation, a new comprehensive statute on sexual assault, Chapter 184, Laws of 1975, 1975 Senate Bill 255, was enacted by the legislature. The law defines four degrees of sexual assault. It focuses on the nature of the coercion employed by the assailant rather than on the degree of resistance shown by the victim. The law became effective in 1976.

In 1977, the Divorce Reform Act, Chapter 105, Laws of 1977, 1977 Assembly Bill 100, was passed by the legislature. The "no-fault" divorce law, as it is often referred to, provides that persons wishing to end their marriage are required to show only that the marriage is "irretrievably broken." The law, which became effective in 1978, also addressed how spousal property is to be divided and how maintenance payments are to be determined. The law has a presumption of equal division of divisible property.

In 1984, Wisconsin became the first state in the nation to adopt a version of the Uniform Marital Property Act, 1983 Wisconsin Act 186, 1983 Assembly Bill 200. Equal property rights of spouses during marriage and when that marriage ends with the death of a spouse were created by adoption of the marital property system. The law became effective January 1, 1986.

The Wisconsin experience demonstrates that it was easier to pass specific legislation to achieve equal rights for women and men than to achieve a more universal constitutional amendment. Even though the Equal Rights Amendment to the state constitution was rejected by the voters in April 1973, the subsequent step-by-step revision of state laws was successful. The 1975 "omnibus bill," the 1975 Sexual Assault law, the 1977 Divorce Reform Act, and the 1984 Marital Property Act collectively established equality of rights for women and men under Wisconsin law.

Part II 🌿

CHAPTER 3 🌿

Property Rights of Spouses in the Territory of Wisconsin, 1836–1850

English Common Law Defined

The English legal system was brought to America by the Pilgrims in 1620, and other English settlers who colonized the Atlantic coast. The legal system established in the colonies became the legal system of the United States after the Declaration of Independence. As the settlers moved westward from the Atlantic seaboard into newly created territories, so did the legal system of English common law. It was the legal system in force when the Territory of Wisconsin was established in 1836.

English common law as a legal system is defined in *Black's Law Dictionary:*

> As distinguished from statutory law created by the enactment of legislatures, the common law comprises the body of those principles and rules of action, relating to the government and security of persons and property, which derive their authority solely from usages and customs of immemorial antiquity, or from the judgments and decrees of the courts, recognizing, affirming, and enforcing such usages and customs; and, in this sense, particularly the ancient unwritten law of England. . . . The 'common law' is all the statutory and case law background of England and the American colonies before the American revolution.[1]

Rules governing the property rights of married persons were an important part of English common law. The "doctrine of coverture" governed the property rights of married women under English common law. The biblical idea that in marriage there is a unity of flesh between husband and wife was the basis for the "doctrine of coverture." The legal meaning of "coverture" was defined by Blackstone, an English legal scholar, in his famous *Commentaries* written in 1765:

> By marriage, the husband and wife are one person in law; that is, the very being or legal existence of the woman is suspended during marriage, or at least is incorporated and consolidated into that of the husband; under whose wing, protection, and cover she performs everything. . . . and her condition during her marriage is called her coverture.[2]

Property Rights of Women

Marital status determined the property rights of a woman under English common law. If a woman was unmarried, a "feme sole," she could manage and control the real and personal property she owned. She could contract with another person. She could sue and be sued. She could sell her real and personal property and keep the proceeds. She could dispose of her property by gift during her lifetime and by will at her death. However, when she married, her property rights and her legal rights were lost or suspended.

A married woman, a "feme covert," retained ownership of the real property (land and buildings) that she owned at the time of marriage or acquired after marriage by gift or inheritance, but she lost the right to manage and control it. Her husband collected the rents or profits, and he did not have to account for them to his wife. If the wife was the first spouse to die, her surviving husband had a life interest called "tenancy by curtesy" in all of her lands, but it was contingent upon a child being born alive to the couple. If the husband was the first spouse to die, the wife regained possession and control of her real property.

A married woman lost ownership of or title to her personal property such as jewelry, clothing, and home furnishings in her possession at the time of marriage. These became her husband's property absolutely and could be sold, taken for his debts, or destroyed by him without his wife's consent. However, "paraphernalia" (as jewelry and clothing were called) could not be willed away from her if her husband was the first spouse to die. The wife regained possession of her paraphernalia at her husband's death if they were still available.

If a married woman owned a particular type of personal property called "choses in action," which consisted of claims against third parties such as stocks, bonds or other sums of money or property recoverable by a law suit, her husband was entitled to absolute ownership of this property if he could obtain possession of it during marriage. To succeed in this effort he was required to obtain permission from the Court of Chancery. (Explained later.)

If a married woman had an income from employment, her husband had control over her earnings.

Marriage, however, gave a married woman certain limited property rights. Her "dower" right entitled her to a life-estate in one-third of all lands owned by her husband during their marriage, but only when and if he was the first spouse to die. During the lifetime of the spouses, a married woman had to join with her husband any time he sold or transferred land in order to release the wife's "dower" right in that land.

A married woman was entitled to financial support by her husband. However, he had the exclusive right to determine the level of support he would provide for her.

If a woman had debts at the time of marriage, her husband was liable for these premarital debts.

When a married woman became a widow, she regained the legal status and property rights of an unmarried woman. Complete dissolution of marriage through the death of the husband removed the "disabilities of coverture," and the widow regained the legal status of a "feme sole."

Dissatisfaction with Married Women's Property Rights

Dissatisfaction with married women's property rights occurred first in England, many years before property rights of married women became a matter of concern in 1846, in the Territory of Wisconsin. In England, legal mechanisms were devised within the English common law system to protect the financial interest of married women. Later in the Territory of Wisconsin, efforts were made to change the legal status of married women and to define their property rights in the state constitution.

In England

Wealthy parents whose daughters brought valuable property to the marriage or later inherited it were dissatisfied with the harshness of the rules governing the property rights of their married daughters. Finding legitimate ways to prevent unscrupulous or incompetent husbands from squandering the property the wife contributed to the marriage was one concern of wealthy parents. Another concern of theirs was to make certain their married daughters had an income during marriage adequate to provide a standard of living similar to that enjoyed in their parental home.

The English Court of Chancery invented ways to protect the income and property rights of a married woman. The Court, often called a Court of Equity, was designed to administer justice in cases where fairness or equity was in question.

Creation of a trust to provide an income for the sole and exclusive use of a married woman was one of the legal devices recognized by the Court. A married woman had the right to use the income from the trust free of her husband's control. A wealthy father could set up funds under the management of a trustee to provide an income for his married daughter.

An "equitable separate estate" was another device recognized by the Court. An "equitable separate estate" was created through an agreement or marriage settlement for the sole benefit of a married woman. Only a wealthy husband or a wealthy father could initiate a marriage settlement.

If the husband petitioned the Court for help in obtaining possession of his wife's particular type of personal property called "choses in action," the Court of Chancery could make its assistance contingent upon the husband's willingness to make a suitable settlement to maintain his wife and children. The settlement required the husband to create an "equitable separate estate" for his wife.

The principal benefit of an "equitable separate estate" was that a married woman could hold property as a "feme sole" free from her husband's control regardless of whether it was real or personal property or both. She could dispose of her "equitable separate estate" by will, gift, transfer or conveyance as long as the instrument creating the estate did not expressly prohibit it.

IN THE TERRITORY OF WISCONSIN

The rules governing the property rights of a married woman in the Territory of Wisconsin were based on English common law. A "feme covert," as a married woman was called, had no legal existence in the eyes of the law separate from her husband. A "feme covert" could not make gifts to her husband, nor could she make contracts or any other legal transaction with him. Neither could she make contracts with others. She could not sue or be sued alone in court. She could not own personal property. Any real estate she owned was under the control of her husband during marriage. She had no right to the custody of her own children. The father was the children's sole guardian during his lifetime and could appoint a guardian by will to the exclusion of the mother's claim.

However, the equity devices recognized by the English Court of Chancery to protect the income and property rights of a married woman were available in the Territory of Wisconsin. A wealthy father could create a trust for the sole benefit of his married daughter. A wealthy husband could arrange a marriage settlement and create an "equitable separate estate" for his wife.

Some men in the Territory of Wisconsin were dissatisfied with the rules governing the property rights of married women. As delegates to the Convention of 1846 called to draft a state constitution, they took the initiative to propose a change in the property laws of Wisconsin.

Why the delegates took this action is unknown. One explanation may be that the social, economic, and political conditions in the United States, particularly on the frontier, differed from those in England where the common law property rules originated.

In the British feudal system, families who owned large tracts of land for generations were the elite. English common law property rules reflected the prevailing social theories of a woman's status in the family, her inherent weakness, and her need for protection. The inferior legal status of married women may have been the result of practical considerations. The property rules simplified legal matters concerning the income and property rights of a married couple, were harmonious with well-established social attitudes, and fitted the patriarchal household.

By contrast, in the United States an abundance of land offered economic opportunity to those who could cope with the hardships of the frontier. An individual's right to accumulate wealth through his or her own effort was paramount in a new nation founded on democratic principles. If a married couple on the frontier was to succeed in acquiring wealth, the joint effort of both husband and wife was required. Recognition of the unfairness of the English common law property rules or the reality of the frontier may have been factors that persuaded some convention delegates to propose a change in property law. Whatever the reason, some men were not only willing but determined to improve the legal status and property rights of married women.

The State Constitution and Married Women's Property Rights

Before a territory such as Wisconsin could become a state and be admitted to the Union, a state constitution, approved by the people in the territory, had to be submitted to and be accepted by the United States Congress. In the Territory of Wisconsin, a constitutional convention was convened in 1846. The constitution drafted by the Convention of 1846 contained a provision that defined the property rights of married women. This was one of several controversial issues that led to its rejection by the voters. This prolonged the process of drafting a constitution the voters in the Territory of Wisconsin would approve.

THE CONVENTION OF 1846

The Convention of 1846 was convened to draft a state constitution in response to the people's desire to change the form of government from territorial status to independent statehood. The Convention met from October 5 to December 16, 1846. There were 125 delegates. No official record of its debates was made. The only official record of its proceedings was the formal daily journal which reported the motions and the votes taken. The journal consisted of 500 pages.

Included in the constitution drafted by the Convention of 1846 was Article XIV "On the Rights of Married Women, And on Exemptions from Forced Sale." It was approved by the Convention delegates by a vote of 61 to 31. Article XIV read:

> Section 1. All property real and personal of the wife, owned by her at the time of her marriage, and also that acquired by her after marriage, by gift, devise, descent or otherwise than from her husband, shall be her separate property. Laws shall be passed providing for the registry of the wife's property and more clearly defining the rights of the wife thereto, as well as to property held by her with her husband, and for carrying out the provisions of this section. Where the wife has a separate

property from that of the husband, the same shall be liable for the debts of the wife contracted before marriage.

Sec. 2. Forty acres of land, to be selected by the owner thereof, or the homestead of a family not exceeding forty acres, which said land or homestead shall not be included within any city or village, and shall not exceed in value one thousand dollars, or instead thereof (at the option of the owner) any lot or lots in any city or village, being the homestead of a family and not exceeding in value one thousand dollars owned and occupied by any resident of this state, shall not be subject to forced sale on execution for any debt or debts growing out of, or founded upon contract, either express or implied, made after the adoption of this constitution. *Provided*, That such exemption shall not affect in any manner any mechanic's or laborer's lien or any mortgage thereon lawfully obtained, nor shall the owner if a married man, be at liberty to alienate such real estate unless by consent of his wife.[3]

Ratification: Political Struggle

The Convention concluded its work on December 16, 1846, and the political battle over ratification began immediately. The territorial press, which devoted much of its space during the 1840's to political issues, was filled with articles and letters debating the merits of the draft constitution. The newspaper editors had a passion for politics. A person submitted an article to the newspaper editor in the hope that it would be published and his viewpoint would have wide public exposure. The popular discussion and debates on Article XIV Section 1. "On the Rights of Married Women" reflected the thinking of men on this issue. Only white men had the right to vote in the Territory of Wisconsin. Milo M. Quaife, Superintendent of the State Historical Society in 1915, described the intensity of the newspaper discussion of the statehood question and the proposed constitution: "For a year and a half the storm of political discussion raged without a lull.[4]

A sampling of some of the arguments used by those who favored Article XIV Section 1. follows. Each excerpt expresses the viewpoint of a different person, except for "b" and "e".

a.   But in looking over the constitution I have been forcibly impressed with the article securing the "rights of married women" as one of great importance, the benefits of which can hardly be foreseen or anticipated. The article, so far as my experience goes, is new, in this country at least. . . .

That woman has long been regarded by the common law as a mere slave (so far as civil privileges are concerned) to her husband's will cannot be denied. . . . There certainly is neither reason nor justice in taking the property which belongs to a single woman and appropriating tomorrow, without her consent and against her own wishes, merely by the will of her husband, simply and only because she has become his wife. Nay, much less is there any good reason why the property which comes to a married woman by descent or devise from her parents or other relatives or friends should at once be taken by her husband and disposed of, and I may say in too many instances utterly dissipated and lost, not only against her wishes and consent, but very frequently leaving her helpless and destitute. . . .

It would seem that no principle of equity or justice is violated by this provision. If any reasonable man will reflect deliberately upon this article, it is confidently believed that he can come to no other conclusion than that it is just, it is right, and should be adopted. . . .[5]

b.   Under the present law if parties intending to become husband and wife think proper, they can provide by marriage settlement contract that the property of the wife shall remain her separate estate, in nowise subject to the husband's control or his creditors. Instances of this kind are not infrequent. . . . But to provide for the wife by marriage settlement requires the employment of a lawyer and the payment to him of a fee of fifteen to fifty dollars. Now all the constitution does is to make the cases uniform and dispense with the lawyer and his fee.[6]

c.   Those conveyances to trustees for the use of married women are in every day's practice; they are on record in perhaps every register's office in the territory; . . . So this much abused section of the constitution, whether wisely placed there or not, seeks to do no more by simple operation of law than may now be done by conveyancing. It merely extends to all a benefit now practically enjoyed only by persons of considerable means.[7]

d.   We seek to restore her to her rights under civil law. We have for nearly two centuries been legislating for man—for ourselves. Let us at last begin to legislate for woman, who has equal rights with man. . . .[8]

e.   But the objectors to this article say that they object to it more for the consequences which will result from it than anything else. They contend . . . that it will dissolve the marriage tie, that it will destroy conjugal affection and fidelity, convert the wife into a termagant, with her separate business, and her pampered "paramour." In other and plainer words, that a little separate property will convert her into a prostitute.[9]

f.   [He] believed the adoption of the section would not have the demoralizing effect mentioned . . . He looked upon the law as it now stands as a remnant of the feudal system, which ought to be abolished, and the sooner the better.[10]

A sampling of arguments used by those who opposed Article XIV Section 1. follows. Each excerpt expresses the viewpoint of a different person.

a.   [He] opposed the section because it was contrary to the usages and customs of society, to the express commands of the Bible that "the twain shall be one flesh"; because it would encourage men to be fraudulent by secreting their property under the cover of the wife's name, and because the provision if adopted will lead the wife to become a speculator, and to engage in all the turmoil and bustle of life, liable to sue and be sued, and thereby destroy her character of a wife; and because villains would be induced to seek wives not for their sake, but for the sake of covering up their frauds.[11]

b.   The laws furnish all needful protection now, when they bind the husband to obtain the consent of his wife before he can dispossess her of her interest in the real estate, when they are so framed that a man can if he chooses leave property in trust for his daughter and her heirs. But even this is not sufficient for those at the present day who arrogate to themselves the peculiar privilege of being champions of woman's rights.[12]

c. In short, we shall see in every family where the wife has property two interests instead of one and that peace and harmony which now so generally reign in the family circle give place to discord and contention. For our part we are not prepared for such a change in the social system as this law will produce; we cannot look quietly on and see the foundation upon which society rests broken up and subverted.[13]

d. [He] led off in an able and calm speech in condemnation of the provisions of the article and in a severe rebuke of the improprieties and turbulence of manner in which it had been discussed and the discourtesy with which its opponents had been treated. He declared . . . if this article were adopted, he should feel it his duty to go home and oppose the constitution.[14]

e. Article XIV, on page 44, on the rights of married women and on exemptions from forced sale . . . it would almost seem useless to occupy your columns in exposing its deformities. But so perfectly outrageous and impolitic are its provisions that one can scarcely let it pass without a mark of his disapprobation. . . . if he [citizen] has the least lingering idea of voting for such an instrument, the adoption of which would fix and fasten upon our state a blighting, withering—nay damning—stain which would turn the honest emigrant from our borders, drive honest and honorable citizens from among us, and leave our state to be the resort and to become the receptacle of rogues, swindlers, scapegoats, scapegallows, and all of the refuse of Pandemonium to congregate and settle in.[15]

A commentary written in 1917, by Louise Phelps Kellogg, a Wisconsin historian, described the character of the constitution drafted by the Convention of 1846 and the political furor that generated its defeat:

. . . The constitution [the Convention of 1846] prepared for the consideration of the people was radical and democratic. Its chief model was the constitution and political practice of

New York, but independence of thought and readiness to ex-
periment were marked characteristics of the convention. The
principal innovations were the banking provisions forbidding
all banks of issue; the judiciary arrangement for an elective
system, and the *nisi pruis* method of state courts; the property
rights of married women; and the exemption of the homestead
from the creditor's claim upon the debtor. The question of
negro suffrage was left for a special referendum, when the
constitution's acceptance should be determined. . . .

The opponents of the instrument were of no one party,
but the Whigs, as representatives of the moneyed and business
class, disapproved of the banking and exemption clauses. . . .
The Liberty men opposed ratification because negro suffrage
was not embodied in the instrument. One faction of the Democrats opposed, apparently because the other faction approved.
The entire territory was divided into pro- and anti- constitution
groups. The banking clause and the married women's property and exemption clauses raised a storm of opposition. The
mass of the people was influenced by the impassioned oratory
of the leaders. Mass meetings were held by both "Friends of
the Constitution" and "Anti-Constitution groups." Songs were
written, liberty poles erected, and the populace was stirred to
the pitch where blows succeeded words as arguments.[16]

The voters were influenced by their party leaders. Many voters did not understand the radical proposals embodied in the constitution, but they were prejudiced against it. Consequently, on
April 6, 1847, the voters rejected the constitution by a vote of 20,231
"no" votes to 14,119 "yes" votes.

THE CONVENTION OF 1847–1848

The desire to have the people of Wisconsin participate in the presidential campaign of 1848 provided the pressure for a new convention. The sole business of an extra session of the Territorial
Legislature in October, 1847, was to arrange for a new constitutional convention. The number of delegates was limited to 69.
Only six members of the first convention were delegates to the
second. Some delegates were instructed by their nominating con-

ventions, and others were closely questioned on the subjects of banking, married women's rights, and exemptions. The convention began on December 15, 1847, and ended on February 2, 1848. After the convention had been in session for a time, a record of the debates was made.

The constitution framed by the second convention was a new draft from preamble to signatures, according to one observer. The constitution was based on general principles to provide the fundamental law of the state. It included a bill of rights omitted from the first one. The "ultra radical" features of the first constitution were dealt with in different ways. The banking article was revised to provide a harmless banking privilege. On the rights of married women and the homestead exemption there was discreet silence. The elective judiciary was the only innovative feature of the first constitution that was unchanged in the second.

The men who were determined to change the rules governing the property rights of married women did not abandon their cause. They merely changed their strategy.

> On the subject of married women's rights and exemptions of real and personal property from forced sale our mind is decided. We are in favor of the first, and of the most liberal provisions in regard to the last. But we care not if the constitution is entirely silent in reference to both, so long as the legislature may have the power to act in the premises. Indeed, considering the progressive state of the public mind on this and kindred subjects, we should prefer to leave this matter to state legislation, without constitutional privilege or restriction, believing that by this means we shall secure from time to time far more liberal provisions than could readily be secured if constitutional provisions always stood in the way of progress and reform. . . . we give them (our conservative and Whig friends) due notice that in the state legislature, as soon as organized, we shall not only show fight, but shall continue the contest until the measures we seek, which we know to be those of the people, and of popular rights, are fully triumphant.[17]

The draft of the second constitution was completed on February 2, 1848, and the popular election for its ratification set for

March. On March 14, 1848, seventy-four percent of the voters approved the constitution by a vote of 16,417 in favor and 6,174 against.

History confirms the success of the strategy. The state constitution was adopted March 14, 1848. The state of Wisconsin was admitted to the Union on May 29, 1848. The first session of the Wisconsin state legislature began on June 5, 1848. Almost two years later, on February 1, 1850, the Wisconsin legislature enacted Chapter 44, Laws of 1850—"An act to provide for the protection of married women in the enjoyment of their own property."

History of the Wisconsin Constitution

The history of the efforts to change the rules governing the property rights of married women made in the Territory of Wisconsin might never have been available to the general public if a documentary history of the state constitution had not been written.

Under the direction of Milo M. Quaife, Superintendent of the State Historical Society, a documentary history of the state constitution was compiled from the sparse official records of the Convention of 1846, and the Convention of 1847, and a unique collection of newspapers published by the territorial press. By 1847, there were about two dozen newspapers in the Territory of Wisconsin. Files for about half of them covering the period of constitutional origin are preserved in the State Historical Library.

Originally the editorial staff planned to compile a comprehensive history of the origin of the state constitution. However, they limited the history "to the immediate period of time in which the constitution of Wisconsin was formulated and admission to statehood gained."[18]

Quaife explained the reason for this decision in the Preface to Volume I of the Constitutional Series:

> In view of the abundance of material available it quickly became evident that a selective principle must be applied to determine what should be included in, and what excluded from, our documentary record. The compilation that has been made does not

aim, therefore, to include all the material which has been at the editors' disposal. It does aim to present everything needful to a clear understanding of the currents of thought and of politics in the period under discussion, and it is believed that henceforth, no one, however specialized his interest may be, need traverse anew the ground we have covered in performing our editorial task.[19]

The thoroughness with which the editorial staff did its work is evidenced by the four-volume Constitutional Series they produced. Volume I, *The Movement Toward Statehood*, was published in 1918. Volume II, *The Convention of 1846*, was published in 1919. Volume III, *The Struggle over Ratification*, was published in 1920, and Volume IV, *The Attainment of Statehood*, was published in 1928.

CHAPTER 4

Property Rights of Spouses in the State of Wisconsin, 1850–1985

Separate Property System— An American Innovation

A new idea about the property rights of spouses was introduced in the United States, and it had a profound effect on the legal system. This American legal innovation was gender specific statutory law that defined the property rights of married women. Replacing the unwritten English common law property rules, the written law rejected the "doctrine of coverture," and restored the legal personality or legal existence of a married woman. The 1850 Wisconsin Statute enacted by the state legislature was one of those American legal innovations.

In the United States, property law is under the jurisdiction of the state, not the federal, government. Hence, the state legislature has the power to change the law governing the property rights of married women. In 1839, American states began one by one to enact statutes that defined the property rights of married women. Collectively these laws were referred to as the Married Women's Property Acts. They varied from state to state.

The intent of the laws defining the property rights of married women was to remove by statute certain, though not all, of the English "common law disabilities" imposed on married women. The "disabilities" meant a married woman did not have

certain legal rights that men and unmarried women had. To remove a "common law disability," a state legislature had to enact a
statute that defined a legal right specifically for married women.

The initial legislative proposals were experiments in drafting
legislation that defined a married woman's property rights. Cau-
tion was exercised. Only one disability was removed at a time.

Kay Ellen Thurman, a University of Wisconsin Law School
graduate student (1966), reviewed all of the Married Women's
Property Acts. Her intensive research included seven states, one
of which was Wisconsin. She studied the language of the Acts and
cited examples of borrowing, such as: "The Oregon (1852) statute
was expressly copied from the New York (1848) provision."[1] She
noted that

> . . . in the relatively short span of fifteen years, statute law pre-
> empted this field of public policy. Quickly there developed a
> standardized pattern of legislation to which custom has
> attached the label of the Married Women's Property Acts.[2]

She states:

> On the whole, the state legislatures did a poor job in formulat-
> ing these statutes. . . . Their focus tended to be on negatives—
> on what a woman should be freed from or protected against.
> This negative approach was responsible for the enactment of a
> series of statutes, each with a relatively narrow focus.[3]

The original statutes simply allowed a married woman to retain ownership of all property, both real and personal, that she
owned before marriage or acquired after marriage by gift or inheritance and exempted it from liability for her husband's debts.
These first statutes did not remove any other "common law disability" of a married woman. As a result the legislatures were required to amend or supersede provisions of these first statutes to
achieve their intended goal.

The process of changing the property rights of married
women was slow and evolutionary. In some states years elapsed
between the removal of one disability and removal of the next.

Thurman noted: "The general Married Women's Property Act in Wisconsin was passed in 1850, but wages were not covered until 1872."[4]

The character of the legislation embodied in the Married Women's Property Acts was described by Thurman:

> ... in large measure legislatures ... failed to discharge their distinctive legislative responsibility of developing rational and orderly generalizations of public policy. Instead, the legislatures developed the law in a manner more like that associated with courts—in a case-by-case fashion, within the context of particular controversies.[5]

Implementing the Married Women's Property Acts was not easy. Disputes over the legality and meaning of the Act occurred, and had to be resolved through litigation.

The constitutionality of the new statutes was challenged in court. Thurman states:

> The most common challenge was predicated on the alleged retroactive effect of the statutes. . . . Courts regularly avoided this issue by interpreting such legislation as intended to have only prospective operation. . . .
>
> A second kind of constitutional challenge to a statute was that it impaired the obligations of the existing marriage contract, contrary to the proscription of the United States Constitution. New York judges met this objection by defining the marriage contract as unique: it was an agreement the terms of which the legislature alone set, under its continuing police power; hence no statutory redefinition of terms could be deemed to impair the marriage contract. . . .[6]

In disputes over the interpretation of the Acts other than the constitutional issues, judges differed in their rulings. Many adopted a restrictive approach holding closely to the statutory language. Others were more expansive or liberal in their approach. Thurman states:

> Although the courts appear to have been unsympathetic to the Married Women's Property Acts, to a large extent this was

probably their response to the problems posed by poor legislative drafting and definition.[7]

Case law was created by the decisions made by judges in their interpretation of the meaning of a statute. Points of law not covered by a statute were governed by English common law principles and by equity doctrines created and enforced by the English Court of Chancery. A litigant had the right of appeal to a higher court. A state's highest court provided the final resolution of some disputes over the property rights of spouses.

The Married Women's Property Acts made a fundamental change in the basic principle underlying property law. The "doctrine of coverture" was rejected. The new legal system that evolved was more compatible with social, economic,and political conditions in the United States than was the English common law property rules. The new property law, called separate property law, treated each spouse as an individual, a separate person.

The Wisconsin Statute: "Property Rights of Married Women"

The portion of Wisconsin laws covering property rights of married women evolved over time. It began in 1850, as Chapter 44, Laws of 1850, "An act to provide for the protection of married women in the enjoyment of their own property."[8] The original statute was limited in scope. Over time, however, Wisconsin law was gradually amended to increase the property rights of married women.

The title of this section of the statutes was changed to clarify its content. In the 1878 revision of the Wisconsin Statutes, the title of the chapter "On Rights of Married Women" was changed to "On Property Rights of Married Women."

The statutes were renumbered from time to time. In 1979, Chapter 246 "Property Rights of Married Women" was renumbered Chapter 766. This statute and its earlier versions governed the property rights of married women in Wisconsin from 1850 through December 31, 1985.

Prior to 1986, Chapter 766 "Property Rights of Married Women" was contained in only two pages, and focused on specific rights and responsibilities of a married woman as the sole owner of separate property.

Prior to 1986, the first three sections (766.01, 766.02, 766.03) defined a married woman's right to own real and personal property acquired before marriage and property received by gift or inheritance after marriage. Her right to manage and control her sole and separate property was defined as "being in the same manner and with like effect as if she were unmarried."[9] And her right to make gifts to her husband, to receive gifts from him and to inherit property from him was defined: "any conveyance, transfer or lien executed by either husband or wife to or in favor of the other shall be valid to the same extent as between other persons."[10] Her sole and separate property was not subject to disposal by her husband nor liable for his debts.

Section 766.05 dealt with a married woman's earnings. To qualify as her sole and separate property, her wage or salary had to be paid by an employer other than her husband.

> The individual earnings of every married woman, *except those accruing from labor performed for her husband, or in his employ or payable by him*, shall be her separate property and shall not be subject to her husband's control or liable for his debts.[11]
> [italics added]

Section 766.06 dealt with a married woman's right to transact business in her own name and for her own benefit under specified conditions.

> When the husband of any married woman has deserted her or for any cause neglects or refuses to provide for her support or for the support and education of the children, *she shall have the right to transact business in her own name and to collect and receive profits of such business, her own earnings and the earnings of her minor children in her charge or under her control and apply the same for her own support and the support and education of such children.* Such business and earnings shall not be subject to her husband's control or interference or liable for his debts.[12]
> [italics added]

Section 766.07 dealt with a married woman's right to sue in her own name.

> Every married woman may sue in her own name and shall have all the remedies of an unmarried woman in regard to her separate property or business and to recover the earnings secured to her by sections 766.05 and 766.06,and shall be liable to be sued in respect to her separate property or business, and judgment may be rendered against her and be enforced against her and her separate property in all respects as if she were unmarried. . . .[13]

Section 766.075 dealt with a married woman's liability for injury to her husband.

> A husband shall have and may maintain an action against his wife for the recovery of damages for injuries sustained to his person caused by her wrongful act, neglect or default.[14]

Section 766.08 made clear that the husband was not liable for his wife's antenuptial debts (debts owed by wife before marriage).

Sections 766.09 and 766.11 dealt with a married woman's right to buy life insurance on the life of her husband, her son or other person and her right to assign an insurance policy.

Section 766.10 dealt with a married woman's right as an assignee or receiver.

Section 766.15 dealt with equal rights of women and men. It was added to Chapter 766 in 1965. (See Chapter 2: History of Equal Rights Legislation.)

The Wisconsin law of 1850 removed some, but not all, of the "common law disabilities" of married women, and the law applied only to the property rights of a married woman. The statute did not change the general status of a married woman or the relationship of husband and wife. Their duties and responsibilities to each other under English common law were not affected. Therefore, in Wisconsin on December 31, 1985, some of the "coverture disabilities" of married women still existed due to the unrepealed English common law rules.

In order to comprehend fully the property rights of a married woman under the separate property system in Wisconsin prior to 1986, a person would need to understand the provisions of Chapter 766, case law and all other Wisconsin statutes that affected the property rights of married women.

Separate Property System Beneficiaries

All married women benefited from the separate property system that restored their legal existence and defined their property rights. In general, married women had the same rights of ownership, management, and control of property as unmarried women. A wife's property rights were improved by giving her the legal right to a separate estate in an ongoing marriage. The right to earn, inherit, and accumulate wealth were legal rights made available to all married women. However, inequities in the separate property system existed.

In Wisconsin the married women who benefited most from the separate property system were those who acquired separate property and retained sole ownership of the property throughout their lifetime. The separate property of a married woman consisted of: 1) property owned before marriage; 2) property acquired by gift or inheritance, including income from a trust established by a third party; 3) earnings from an employer other than her husband. To accumulate wealth independently, a married woman had to put her self-interest ahead of other considerations. Only if she retained title to her separate property in her name alone did she have rights to manage and control her separate estate. A married woman had to avoid pooling her earnings with those of her husband and comingling or mixing her other separate property with property of her husband if she wanted to retain a separate estate.

As the sole owner of property, a married woman had access to credit in her own name just like any other property owner and had the right to dispose of her separate property by will at death. After the Married Women's Property Acts, married women who established and maintained a separate estate had a certain amount of financial independence during marriage and some economic security throughout their lifetime.

The Marriage Contract

The state has jurisdiction over the legal aspects of marriage. In Wisconsin prior to 1986, the law governing the marriage contract contributed to the inequities associated with the property rights of spouses. The unique characteristics of the marriage contract were unfamiliar or unknown to the average person. When they married, many couples assumed that in their new partnership venture they had the freedom to share their legal duties and responsibilities in a way that best suited their lifestyle.

The law viewed the marriage contract differently. Although the marriage contract was not available in writing for the couple to review, the marriage contract required husband and wife to do certain limited things for one another. In general, the husband was responsible for the financial support of the family, while the wife was expected to provide homemaking, child care, and sexual services. Furthermore, the courts were rigid in their interpretation of these marital roles.

The state exercises its authority to define marriage and the terms of the marriage contract through statutes enacted by the state legislature and court decisions. Chapter 765 of the Wisconsin Statutes "Marriage" states:

> Marriage, so far as its validity at law is concerned, is a civil contract, to which consent of the parties capable in law of contracting is essential, and which creates the legal status of husband and wife.[15]

Chapter 765 makes clear that marriage is a civil contract. However, the pre-1986 statute did not define the terms of the marriage contract. In Wisconsin prior to the Marital Property Act, the terms of the marriage contract were not set down in writing in any one place. The marriage contract provisions were explained little by little over the years in court cases and statutes. Because the relevant court cases and statutes were scattered and not easy to locate, most people married without ever knowing to what they had legally committed themselves. For some married women it was a harsh experience to discover the inequities in the separate property system that stemmed from the marriage contract.

The marriage contract is unique because there are three parties to a marriage contract—the bride, the groom, and the state. State approval is required to make a marriage contract (marriage license), and state certification is required to end a marriage contract—if by death of a spouse a death certificate, if by divorce a court decree. The marriage contract is unique in another respect. The parties to the contract do not negotiate the terms of the contract because the state defines the terms of the marriage contract.

Inequities Associated with Separate Property Rights of Spouses

The inequities associated with the property rights of spouses under the separate property system were many. Each kind of inequity is addressed separately. The economic consequences of marriage, particularly for women, sometimes created unexpected economic hardships. The cumulative effect of these inequities made many married women aware of the unequal property rights of spouses in Wisconsin.

FAMILY FINANCIAL DECISIONS

Prior to 1986 in Wisconsin a married woman had no legal right to participate in family financial decisions if her husband was the only wage earner in the family. He was the sole owner of his earnings and had the exclusive right to manage and control the property bought with his earnings. He was not obligated to inform his wife about the financial decisions he made. If a married woman was, also, a full-time or part-time wage earner, she had no voice in financial decisions relating to her husband's earnings. If a married woman's husband invited her to share in family financial matters, his action was strictly voluntary, not a legal requirement, and he could revoke the invitation at any time.

A MARRIED WOMAN'S ACCESS TO CREDIT

Creditworthiness, the financial ability to pay the creditor, determined a married woman's access to credit. If she did not own property in her own name and was a full-time, unpaid worker in the home, a married woman was not creditworthy. Prior to 1986 in Wisconsin her husband had to sign her credit application and indicate a willingness to pay for the credit extended to his wife under the circumstances. Because a married woman had no legal interest in her husband's income and property, she had no legal right to obligate or encumber his separate property. If a married woman owned separate property or worked for wages, she had access to credit in her own name based upon her earnings and property, just like any male property owner.

A MARRIED WOMAN'S RIGHT TO SUPPORT

In Wisconsin prior to 1986, a married woman's right to support was an issue that was never comprehensively addressed. The husband had an obligation to support his wife, but he had the exclusive right to determine the level of support he would provide for his wife. If he did not provide a reasonable or adequate level of support, a married woman had no effective legal means of enforcing her right to an acceptable level of living as long as she was living with her husband in an ongoing marriage.

An example of this inequity comes from Nebraska. The couple's home had no bathroom, bathing facilities, inside toilet, or kitchen sink. Hard and soft water were obtained from a well and a cistern. The furnace had not been in good working order for five or six years, and at age 66, and after three abdominal operations, Mrs. McGuire was tired of scooping coal and ashes. The heater in their 1929 Ford did not work well. Her husband, nearly

80 years of age, had assets valued at more than $200,000 and a yearly income between $8,000 and $9,000 from interest on bonds and rent from real estate. Mrs. McGuire sued her husband in a Nebraska state court, asking the court to order him to provide a new car and needed facilities in their home. The Nebraska Supreme Court decision in 1953 (*McGuire v. McGuire*) states:

> The living standards of a family are a matter of concern for the household and not for the courts to determine, even though the husband's attitude . . . leaves little to be said in his behalf. As long as the home is maintained and the parties are living as husband and wife it may be said that . . . the purpose of the marriage relation is being carried out. Public policy requires such a holding.[16]

This court decision established an important precedent for viewing support as a "private" family matter, thus preventing women from exercising their rights. Case law from any state with a statute having language and substantive provisions similar to a Wisconsin statute may be used in resolving a conflict over the property rights of a married woman. Hence, it was highly likely that a Wisconsin court would have followed this precedent before 1986.

The "doctrine of necessaries" was used to provide some indirect financial support for a wife. The "doctrine of necessaries" began as an English common law rule based upon the husband's duty to support himself and his wife. It made the husband liable to creditors for food, clothing, medical care, etc., furnished voluntarily by a creditor to him or his wife.

In three separate decisions (*Sharp Furniture Inc. v. Buckstaff*, 1980); (*Estate of Stromsted*, 1980); (*Marshfield Clinic v. Discher*, 1982), the Wisconsin Supreme Court interpreted the "doctrine of necessaries" to mean the husband was primarily liable and the wife was secondarily liable for "necessaries" obtained by either from a creditor. Even if the wife did not incur the debt and did not have possession of the goods, such as a car, she was secondarily liable. This meant the creditor was required to attempt to collect the debt first from the husband. If the creditor was not successful, then the creditor could attempt to collect from the wife. An irony of these decisions was that the court made the wife liable for the debt even if she was not a wage-earning spouse, but the court did not give her any legal right of ownership in her husband's income or property acquired during marriage.

A Married Woman's Earnings

In Wisconsin prior to 1986, if a married woman was paid a wage or salary by an employer other than her husband, her earnings were her separate property. If she was paid a wage or salary by her husband for work she performed in a solely owned family enterprise such as a farm or small commercial business, her earnings were *not* her separate property, with one exception, described later.

Chapter 766 of the Wisconsin Statutes 1981-1982 stated:

> The individual earnings of every married woman, *except those accruing from labor performed for her husband, or in his employ or payable by him,* shall be her separate property and shall not be subject to her husband's control or liable for his debts.[17] [italic added]

Statutory and case law in Wisconsin prior to 1986 considered a wife's labor in her husband's business or on a farm as a "wifely duty" or domestic service. Her husband was entitled to all profits from her labor in their mutual enterprise or in the home.

There was one exception to this rule. If the family enterprise was a legally created business partnership with a written partnership agreement between husband and wife, and if self-employment taxes were paid for both spouses, and if the firm's financial records showed the profits from the business were divided between husband and wife, then the earnings of each spouse qualified as separate property.

A Married Woman's Liability
for Husband's Debts

Creditors could not force a married woman to satisfy her husband's debts from her separate property unless she co-signed an instrument of debt with him. Extension of credit to a married man was sometimes made contingent upon his wife's willingness to be a co-signer. This was a practice adopted by financial institutions to insure that various actions by the husband, such as transfer of his property to his wife as a gift, were not used to defeat the claims of creditors.

Joint and individual liability was created when a married woman co-signed a debt instrument with her husband. This meant the income or property, or both, of either or both spouses could be reached to satisfy the debt. The 1891 Wisconsin Supreme Court decision (*Nelson v. MacDonald*) states:

> By signing a joint note with her husband the wife clothes him with prima facie evidence of her intention to charge her separate estate, and cannot deny such intention as against an innocent holder of the note who advanced money upon the faith thereof. She is therefore liable to a personal judgment.[18]

A married woman as a co-signer might not know the legal responsibilities or financial risks she was taking unless the meaning of joint and individual liability had been explained to her. If she was gainfully employed, the creditors could take her earnings first to satisfy the debt. If she owned property acquired by gift or inheritance, that property could be reached by the creditors and taken first to satisfy the obligation, if the creditor chose to do so. Wisconsin had no legal requirement that the income and property of the husband who initiated the debt be taken first to satisfy the debt. A married woman had no legal recourse to recover from her husband the amount of her earnings or her solely owned property taken to satisfy a debt. As a result, a wife who co-signed an indebtedness note unintentionally made a gift to her husband from her separate estate whenever the latter was used to satisfy her husband's debts unless he voluntarily reimbursed her.

If a divorced woman co-signed a debt instrument with her husband before the divorce, she continued to be liable for the unsatisfied debt after their divorce. Even though the husband had agreed to pay the debt as a part of the divorce settlement or order, the creditors could collect from the divorced wife all payments due to satisfy the debt. The former wife would then have to try to collect such payments from her former husband.

Co-ownership of Property

Property held by a document of title listing the names of the husband and wife as "tenants-in-common" or as "joint tenants" creates co-ownership property. Under the separate property system, a document of title, if one exists, determines the ownership of property.

When property is held as "tenants-in-common" with the names of both husband and wife on the document of title, then during their lifetime each spouse has an equal, undivided interest in the ownership of the property. Each spouse has the right to will one-half of the property at death. In the absence of a valid will, the deceased spouse's one-half interest in the "tenancy-in-common" passes under the laws of intestacy.

When property is held as "joint tenants" with the names of both husband and wife on the document of title, then during the lifetime of the "joint tenants," each has an equal, undivided interest in the property with the right of survivorship. At the death of one spouse, the decedent's interest is automatically owned by operation of law by the surviving spouse. Neither spouse has the right to will property held in "joint tenancy."

Under Wsiconsin law, during their lifetime, either joint tenant may "sever" the "joint tenancy." One joint tenant has the legal right to unilaterally (without consent or knowledge of the other joint tenant) divide the "joint tenancy" and eliminate the survivorship right of the other joint tenant. Notification of the other joint tenant of the action taken is not required. The severance action changes the form of ownership from "joint tenants" to "tenants-in-common" in which each tenant owns an equal, undivided interest in the property without survivorship. A surviving spouse may discover at the death of her husband that she owns only one-half, not the entire property which was originally held in "joint tenancy." Except for a homestead, which is governed by a special rule, all property held in "joint tenancy" by husband and wife is at risk of unilateral severance.

GIFTS AND DONATIVE INTENT

Sometimes a married woman learned about the rules governing gifts and donative intent too late to remedy the financial injustice it imposed upon her. Prior to 1986, in Wisconsin, if a married woman pooled her earnings or other property with those of her husband for the benefit of the family in an account titled only in her husband's name, she probably was not aware of the financial risk she was taking. The legal interpretation of her action was that she had made a gift to her husband by making such transfers into her husband's account, since these transfers fulfilled the gift law requirement of donative intent.

In this situation, the married woman suffered a financial loss equal to the sum of her contributions unless her name was also on the document of title to property acquired during marriage. Thus a wife was economically penalized by the law for helping to support her own family by pooling her earnings unless her name was on the document of title.

NO INHERENT RIGHT OF WIFE IN
HUSBAND'S PROPERTY

In Wisconsin prior to 1986, marriage in and of itself did not create for the wife an inherent right to share in the income and property acquired during marriage by her husband. A Wisconsin Supreme Court decision made this very clear. A homemaker, through frugal management of the household allowance given to her by her husband, saved small amounts of money which she deposited in two savings accounts held in her name in trust for their sons. At her death her husband challenged her right of ownership to the funds in these savings accounts, and thus their sons' rights to receive the savings accounts' funds.

The Wisconsin Supreme Court decision in 1966 (*Rasmussen v. Oshkosh Savings and Loan*) states:

> Gifts from a husband to his wife are not presumed from the marital relationship but are governed by the same rules as gifts between strangers ... The general rule in separate property states ... is that the excess left after paying the joint expense of ... the family remains the property of the husband....[19]

In this case the husband was the sole wage earner. The court ruled that any savings from the household allowance was the separate property of the husband. The decision of the court was explicit in stating that in Wisconsin there was no legal requirement for sharing income and property by husband and wife during marriage, even when the savings resulted from a wife's frugal management of the family's household allowance.

Property Disposition at Death of Spouse

In addition to the inequities experienced by a married woman during an ongoing marriage, some inequities existed which were related to the disposition of property at the death of a spouse. One stemmed from the right of the owner spouse to choose to dispose of property by either probate or nonprobate methods. Another was the right of the surviving spouse to share in the property, which was acquired by the couple during marriage subject to probate administration. The laws of intestacy governed the distribution of the decedent's estate subject to probate administration if a spouse failed to make a will.

RIGHT OF SPOUSE TO WILL PROPERTY

Both spouses had the right to dispose of property owned at death by will in Wisconsin prior to 1986. In fact, the first property right provided for a married woman under Wisconsin law was the right to make a will under specified conditions.

Chapter 66, Laws of 1849, Section 1 states:

> Every person of full age and sound mind . . . may devise or dispose of the same by his last will and testament in writing . . . and any married woman may devise and dispose of any real or personal property held by her, or to which she is entitled in her own right, by her last will and testament in writing, and may alter or revoke in like manner that a person under no disability may do the same: *Provided, that no such will, alteration or revocation shall be of any validity without the consent of the husband of such married woman, in writing, annexed to such will, alteration or revocation, and attested and subscribed, and to be proven and recorded in like manner as a last will and testament is required to be witnessed, proven and recorded.*[20]
> [italic added]

Ten years later, in 1859, the legislature amended the statute by revoking the proviso. As a result of this amendment, a married woman obtained the right to make a will without her husband's consent to dispose of her separate estate.

A married woman's separate estate consisted of: 1) property owned before marriage; 2) property acquired by gift including any gifts from her husband; 3) property acquired by inheritance; 4) property acquired with her earnings paid by an employer other than her husband. A married woman had the right to will: 1) property in her name alone; 2) her interest in property that she voluntarily titled in the names of both husband and wife as "tenants-in-common"; 3) her interest in property that her husband voluntarily titled in the names of both husband and wife as "tenants-in-common."

A married woman could not will any part of the property acquired by her husband during marriage except that which her husband voluntarily titled in her name alone or in the names of both husband and wife as "tenants-in-common."

A married man, as the wage earner spouse, had the right to dispose of all property acquired by the couple during marriage except that which he voluntarily titled in his wife's name alone or in the names of both husband and wife as "tenants-in-common."

If a spouse died without a will, the decedent's separate estate subject to probate administration was disposed of according to Wisconsin laws of intestacy.

Surviving Spouse's Right in Decedent's Estate

The legal rules protecting the right of a surviving spouse to share in the estate of the deceased spouse changed over time in the United States and in Wisconsin. The "dower" right of a wife to a life estate in all lands owned by her husband during their marriage and the "tenancy by courtesy" right of the husband in the land of his deceased wife were significant rights of the surviving spouse when land was the principal asset acquired by a couple during marriage. With the shift in population from farming to nonfarm occupations, however, the importance of land as the major family asset declined, and the importance of new forms of investment such as corporate stock, government bonds, savings accounts, etc., increased. In the mid-20th century probate codes were reformed to deal effectively with the new kinds of assets a married couple accumulated during marriage. The concept of "elective" share, which applied to personal property as well as to real estate owned by a spouse, replaced the land-specific "dower" right of the wife and the "tenancy-by-curtesy" right of the husband.

Typically, as in Wisconsin prior to 1986, the "elective" share was a surviving spouse's right to elect one-third of the decedent's net probate estate, even when the property was willed to others. Some married women assumed the "elective" share applied to the total wealth of the deceased spouse. This assumption was erroneous and for some married women created a false sense of economic security. The net probate estate was the amount that remained in the decedent's probate estate after all creditors' claims against the decedent's estate and other expenses had been satisfied. In addition, a will governed only the decedent's property subject to probate administration.

During her/his lifetime, the owner spouse had the right to transfer as much property as she/he chose to by nonprobate methods. These methods included: 1) creating by document of title a "joint tenancy" with a third party (a child, for instance); 2) creating a trust for the benefit of someone other than her/his spouse (a parent, for instance); 3) using a P. O. D (payable-on-death) to a third party to name the beneficiary on government bonds, savings accounts, and certificates of deposit; 4) naming someone other than her/his spouse as the beneficiary of her/his life insurance policy. In most states, including Wisconsin, if the owner spouse chose any of these methods, the amount of property subject to probate could be significantly reduced. Most surviving spouses were widows, not widowers. If the husband's probate estate was materially reduced by nonprobate transfers of property, the widow's share of his probate estate based on her "elective" share was reduced accordingly.

The probate estate was liable for the decedent's debts including: 1) burial expenses; 2) the administrative costs of closing the estate; 3) both federal and state taxes. If the probate estate was insufficient to cover these obligations, the net probate estate was zero. In this case, the surviving spouse's right to an "elective" share of the decedent's net probate estate was meaningless.

If the decedent's net probate estate was zero, either because the debts exceeded the assets or there was little or nothing in the probate estate because of nonprobate transfers to third persons, the husband had effectively disinherited his wife. The "elective" share best protected the right of the widow when all or most of her deceased husband's property was subject to probate. Regardless of how many years the couple had been married, the typical widow's "elective" share was limited to one-third of the decedent's net probate estate. This was the law in Wisconsin prior to 1986.

Wisconsin Laws of Intestacy

In Wisconsin, prior to 1986, if a spouse died without a will (intestate) and there were no children, the surviving spouse inherited the entire net probate estate. If there were only children of the marriage, the surviving spouse inherited the first $25,000 of the estate and one-half of the balance if the decedent spouse left one child, or one-third of the balance if the decedent spouse left two or more children. If the deceased spouse had any surviving children by a prior marriage, or issue of such children, the surviving spouse did not receive the first $25,000 but divided the estate with all the decedent's children: half, if the decedent left only one child; one-third, if the decedent left two or more children.

Impact of Separate Property System on Transfer Taxes

Tax laws generally reflect property ownership laws. In Wisconsin, the impact of the federal estate tax and of the Wisconsin inheritance tax on the surviving spouse frequently focused the attention of married women on the inequities of the tax laws, rather than on the inequities of the separate property system.

FEDERAL TRANSFER TAXES

The federal government imposes a transfer tax on property transferred by the owner to others. If the transfer occurs during the lifetime of the property owner, the federal transfer tax is called a gift tax. If the transfer occurs by reason of death, the federal transfer tax is called an estate tax and is based on the size of the decedent's taxable estate. The tax is paid by the decedent's estate. Federal gift and estate tax laws are gender neutral.

Federal estate and gift tax laws were changed after World War II. The changes were designed to equalize federal taxes on the transfer of property by the owner spouse in both separate property states and community property states. Before 1948, in community property states, generally property acquired during marriage due to the efforts of either or both spouses was owned equally by both spouses. At the death of either spouse, only one-half of the property acquired during marriage was included in the decedent's taxable estate which determines federal estate taxes. In the separate property states, the property acquired during marriage generally was the property of the wage or income earner. Hence, if the sole or primary earner died first, all of the property acquired during acquired during marriage was included in the taxable estate of the decedent owner spouse and was subject to the federal estate tax, unless the surviving spouse, usually the widow, could prove a monetary contribution to the acquisition of the property.

In 1948, Congress enacted a law that eliminated these regional inequities and provided for the use of a limited marital deduction in separate property states. The property owner spouse could, in her/his will, transfer a maximum of $250,000 or one-half of the adjusted gross value of his estate to his widow or her widower tax free, if the surviving spouse received outright title to the property. Funds left in trust for the widow also qualified for the limited marital deduction, if the widow could receive all the trust income for life and had the unrestricted power to dispose of the property at her death. This provision reduced the size of the decedent's estate subject to federal estate tax by one-half in estates of $500,000 or less.

In 1976, the Federal Tax Reform Act provided that the husband could make a tax-free "gift" to his wife of one-half of the property held in "joint tenancy," up to a value of the first $100,000. As a result of the "gift," the property held in "joint tenancy" by husband and wife would be treated as belonging 50 percent to each spouse, and "fractional shares" would be used in computing each decedent spouse's federal estate tax.

Prior to December 31, 1976, in separate property states the total value of property held in "joint tenancy" by husband and wife was included in the federal taxable estate of the first spouse to die, unless the surviving spouse, typically a widow, could prove a monetary contribution or that the property was acquired by gift or inheritance from a third party. If the widow could establish the necessary proof, only the decedent's undivided share of the "joint tenancy" property was included in the decedent's federal taxable estate.

As a general rule, the "contribution rule" imposed a hardship on the widow in separate property states like Wisconsin. The economic value of the unpaid services performed by the wife in the home and/or the family enterprise was not recognized as a monetary contribution for federal estate tax purposes. Adequate financial records on property gifted to or inherited by the wife were typically unavailable. Hence, the actual monetary contribution made by the widow to the acquisition of property during marriage was difficult to prove.

Other Changes in Federal Transfer Tax Laws

An integrated federal estate and gift tax system was initiated January 1, 1977, and phased in over a ten-year period. As of January 1, 1987, a unified tax credit applies to the decedent's lifetime and testamentary post-death transfers. There is no federal estate or gift tax liability on an individual's taxable estate of $600,000 or less. If the individual's estate exceeds $600,000, a progressive tax rate applies. It begins at 37 percent and increases to 55 percent.

In 1981, Congress eliminated federal gift and estate taxes on interspousal transfers of property during life and at death. In 1982, Congress changed the limited marital deduction to an unlimited marital deduction in both separate and community property states. The annual gift tax exclusion from Federal Gift Tax is $10,000. This amount was set by Congress in 1985. Although the size of the annual exclusion is limited, the number of tax-free gifts a person may make in one year to different donees is unlimited.

Wisconsin Transfer Taxes

The transfer tax imposed by Wisconsin on the recipient's receipt of property transferred at death by the owner is called an inheritance tax. The decedent's estate was liable for the inheritance tax, but if unpaid, was a lien on the property transferred to the person who inherited the property. The recipient was then liable for the inheritance tax. The Wisconsin transfer or inheritance tax was based on the relationship of the decedent to those receiving the decedent's taxable estate. In theory, Wisconsin inheritance laws treated both spouses the same. In practice, the order of death affected the surviving spouse's tax liability. Typically, the widow as the surviving spouse had a greater tax

liability than the widower as the surviving spouse, largely because of the widow's difficulty in proving a monetary contribution to her husband's estate.

Doris Kersten, a Wisconsin farm widow, challenged the Wisconsin Department of Revenue in court on the amount of inheritance tax she paid on a farm she and her deceased husband
owned in "joint tenancy." She argued that the farm was half hers,
and she should pay tax only on the half owned by the decedent.
She and her husband held the farm in "joint tenancy" by document of title from the date of purchase. Throughout their 25
years of married life she helped her husband with every kind of
farm work, in addition to running the household and raising
four children.

The trial court agreed with the widow. The Wisconsin Department of Revenue appealed the decision. On March 2, 1976,
the Wisconsin Supreme Court ruled:

> We agreed with the trial court holding that the continuing con-
> tribution of Doris Kersten in services, industry and skills to
> the operation of the farm enterprise constituted contribution
> in "money's worth" in the production of joint income used to
> acquire jointly held assets involved in the trial court's order.[21]

The Kersten decision made it clear for Wisconsin inheritance
tax purposes that it was not necessary to establish a specific monetary value on the services or contributions rendered to prove they
constituted adequate and full consideration for the survivor's interest in property held jointly. The test for adequacy was the nature and extent of services rendered or contributions made by
the wife as a joint tenant. As a result of the court decision, Mrs.
Kersten was obligated to pay state inheritance tax only on the
decedent's one-half interest in the farm and was entitled to a
refund. The decision was silent, however, on the economic value
of the services performed in the home by the wife. The decision
was also silent on the economic value of the wife's services in a
business that was not held jointly.

In Wisconsin, the husband typically paid no inheritance tax

on property held jointly by husband and wife, if the wife was the first spouse to die.

The Wisconsin legislature made changes in the inheritance tax law that became effective on July 1, 1976. One was the "fractional interest" rule, which applied to completed transfers of property between spouses. By law, only the decedent's one-half interest in jointly held property was included in the decedent's taxable estate. By statutory definition, property held by document of title as "joint tenants" or as "tenants-in-common" by husband and wife were completed transfers of property. However, the "contribution rule" continued to apply to other transfers. Property that required the signature of only one spouse to transfer an asset such as a joint checking account or joint savings account was defined as an incompleted transfer. A transfer of funds into such a joint account by one spouse was not considered a completed gift to the other spouse until the other spouse withdrew funds or wrote a check on the account. If the surviving spouse could prove a monetary contribution to the asset, the proportion contributed by her/him was excluded from the decedent spouse's taxable estate.

In 1978, the Wisconsin tax law was changed to exclude the decedent's one-half interest in property held jointly by husband and wife from the decedent's taxable estate. This exclusion reduced the size of the decedent's taxable estate and lowered the inheritance tax rates for all heirs, including the surviving spouse. In 1979, the personal exemption from inheritance tax for the surviving spouse was increased from $50,000 to $250,000. The tax rate on an interspousal transfer at death was progressive, with a 5 percent rate on property in excess of $250,000, increasing to 6.25 percent on property in excess of $500,000. Wisconsin transfer taxes on interspousal transfers of property during life and at death were eliminated on July 1, 1982. The Wisconsin inheritance tax was phased out over a four-year period, beginning January 1, 1988, and was completely eliminated on January 1, 1992. On January 1, 1992, the Wisconsin Estate Tax became the only transfer tax on property transfers at death. The Wisconsin Estate Tax does not increase the total amount of taxes paid by the decedent's estate.

Under federal law, each state may retain a portion of the federal estate tax from a decedent's estate equal to the state inheritance tax. In effect, the Wisconsin Estate Tax is limited to sums otherwise payable to the federal Internal Revenue Service. It is sometimes called a "pick-up" or "gap" tax, and is a source of revenue for the state.

The Wisconsin gift tax on transfers of property made by the property owner during her/his lifetime was a tax on property transferred without adequate and full consideration. The donor paid the gift tax. Two tax-free gifts were permitted: 1) the "once in a lifetime" exemption; 2) the annual exemption. The lifetime marital exemption was $100,000, and it applied to all gifts between husband and wife during their lifetime. On July 1, 1982, the gift tax on interspousal transfers of property was eliminated. The annual exemption was limited in size, but unlimited in the number of tax-free gifts the property owner could make each year to different recipients or donees. The annual exemption was increased from $1,000 to $3,000 in 1972, and increased to $10,000 in 1985. The Wisconsin gift tax was phased out over a four-year period beginning January 1, 1988. Gifts made on or after January 1, 1992, are not subject to a Wisconsin gift tax. However, the Federal Gift Tax still applies. The annual tax-free gift allowed by federal law is $10,000 per recipient.

Size of Transfer Tax

The size of the decedent's taxable estate for calculation of federal estate tax and Wisconsin inheritance tax was affected by the title-based and contribution-based separate property system. Typically, the decedent spouse was the husband, and the surviving spouse was the wife. The intent of the changes in the federal transfer tax laws in the 1970s and 1980s was to reduce or minimize the amount of transfer taxes paid by the decedent's estate in separate property states like Wisconsin. If the husband took affirmative action to use the new provisions of the federal laws governing transfer taxes, the inequities in separate property states were reduced. If he was unwilling to take the necessary affirmative action, the in-equities were perpetuated.

The federal and state transfer tax laws in effect on the date of the husband's death determined the size of the decedent's federal taxable estate and the amount of Wisconsin inheritance tax paid by the widow as the surviving spouse. From personal experience, many Wisconsin widows were acutely aware of transfer taxes im-posed on property transferred at the death of the husband.

Perceptions of the Separate Property System

A married woman's personal experience, and the personal experiences of other close married female relatives and friends, influenced her perception of the separate property system, and whether or not the law had deficiencies.

Some married men acted as if husband and wife were equal partners in all economic aspects of marriage. There was full dis-closure of the couple's financial affairs, and financial decisions were jointly made. Ownership of income and property acquired during marriage was shared by having a joint bank account and by holding property either in "joint tenancy" or as "tenants-in-common" with the names of both husband and wife on the docu-ments of title. Voluntary actions taken by the husband, typically the spouse owning more property, created equal property rights for husband and wife. Among these couples the wife, assuming the husband was the spouse owning more property, probably was not aware of any deficiencies in the separate property system dur-ing marriage, although equal partnership required voluntary de-liberate actions by the spouse owning more property. Alterna-tively, if the wife (when she was the nonwage or lesser-wage earning spouse), insisted on having her name on the document of title to property acquired during marriage and her husband agreed, co-ownership of property was created. This voluntary action taken by the property owner spouse resulted in both spouses sharing the ownership of property acquired during marriage.

However, if a married woman was not successful in persuading her husband to add her name to the document of title to property acquired during marriage, she had no legal recourse. In addition, the financial position of the widow as the surviving spouse could be severely damaged if the sole proprietor of the family enterprise, such as a farm or small business, created a "joint tenancy" by document of title with a third party, such as a son or daughter, or brother. At the death of the sole proprietor, ownership of the family enterprise would transfer by operation of law to the surviving joint tenant. Since the sole proprietor had the exclusive right to manage and control the property acquired during his lifetime, the husband could take this action without informing his wife. At his death his widow would learn that such nonprobate transfers of property were legal, and the principal asset of the family was not a part of the decedent's probate estate. Hence, the widow could not claim her "elective" share in the family asset she had helped to create by working in the family enterprise during her married life.

The voluntary action, or the lack thereof, taken by the property owner spouse, typically the husband, determined the economic consequences of marriage for his spouse and his widow. As a result, many married women's own personal experiences influenced their perception of the separate property system and emphasized its deficiencies.

Legal Bases of Unequal Separate Property Rights of Spouses

The de facto unequal property rights of spouses in Wisconsin prior to 1986 were created by law and tradition. The basic principle underlying the separate property system was: the wage earner was the sole owner of her/his earnings and had the exclusive right to manage and control the property acquired with those earnings. The name of the spouse on the document of title to property determined ownership of that property. Where there was no document of title, ownership was determined by which spouse supplied the funds to acquire the asset (unless a gift was made and all the requirements of gift law were met). This title-based and contribution-based property system viewed and treated husband and wife in an ongoing marriage as separate individuals. There was no legal requirement that husband and wife share the income and property accumulated by their efforts during marriage.

The spouse who worked full-time in the home for the benefit of the family had no money income from employment. Hence, such a wife traditionally was described as the nonwage earning spouse. Without a money income, the nonwage earning spouse could not accumulate separate property unless it was inherited or gifted to her. As a result, the nonwage earning spouse was a dependent of the wage earner spouse.

Social attitudes reflecting the role of men and women in a marriage relationship were consciously or unconsciously incorporated into statutes and judicial decisions governing the property rights of spouses. Traditional English common law clearly supported the patriarchal family in the "doctrine of coverture" and the notion of "natural male dominance." The idea that women were considered in many ways the private property of men was embodied and perpetuated in marriage under traditional English common law.

In the United States, enactment of the Married Women's Property Acts changed the legal concept of a married woman from that of being her husband's property to being his dependent. The U.S. Supreme Court decision in 1908 *Muller v. Oregon* states:

> Still again, history discloses the fact that woman has always been dependent upon man. He established his control at the outset by superior physical strength, and this control in various forms, with diminishing intensity, has continued to the present. . . . Though limitations upon personal and contractual rights may be removed by legislation, there is that in her disposition and habits of life which will operate against a full assertion of those rights.[22]

Traditionally the role of men was to be the provider for the family. This male provider role was embodied in separate property law. It specified that the husband was responsible for the support of his wife and gave him the exclusive right to define the level of living he would provide for his wife and family.

Ownership of property and gender were the legal bases for one spouse (the husband) having authority over the other spouse (the wife) in the economic aspects of marriage in states with a background of English common law. Statutory law, judicial decisions and tradition confirmed the unequal property rights of spouses in a separate property system.

Two Different Property Systems in the United States

In the United States two different legal systems govern the property rights of spouses. One is the separate property system. The other is the community property system. The separate property system, based on English common law, became the dominant system (42 states) due to historic events. The primary pattern of exploration and settlement within the United States was from east to west. As the population moved west into newly created territories, the legal system based on English common law spread westward. As new states emerged from these territories, the states adopted the established separate property system.

The community property system with a heritage in Spanish and Napoleonic codes was transplanted in the New World by Spanish and French settlers. Some of the southern and western states emerged from the land area formerly owned by Mexico where community property was the established legal system. The Republic of Texas retained the community property system after its emancipation from Mexico in 1836. Out of the territory ceded to the United States by Mexico in 1848 the states of California, Nevada, Arizona, and New Mexico emerged. In 1867 and 1869, the territorial legislatures of Idaho and Washington adopted the community property system based on the California model. In Louisiana, the community property system was based on both French and Spanish law. In these eight states community property was the legal system in force when the states were admitted to the Union.

The community property system recognizes husband and wife as equal owners of community property. The contribution in the form of services or money or both has equal economic value. All property acquired during marriage through the efforts of either or both spouses is community property. However, under traditional community property rules the husband had the exclusive right to manage and control all the community property during his lifetime. Property acquired before and after marriage by one spouse by gift or inheritance is the separate property of that spouse and subject to that spouse's management and control.

Unlike the separate property system based on English common law, there is no single community property system. Each of the eight community property states share some common rules, but also have some separate and distinct rules.

American Women's Criticism of the Law Governing the Property Rights of Spouses

Criticism by American women of the law governing the property rights of spouses in states with a legal system based on English common law began in the colonies and continued with varying degrees of intensity at different points in time for the next two hundred years.

In 1776, Abigail Adams wrote to her husband John, who was helping to draft the Declaration of Independence:

> . . . in the new Code of laws . . . I desire you would remember the Ladies, and be more generous and favorable to them than your ancestors. Do not put such unlimited power into the hands of the Husbands.[23]

John described Abigail's letter as "saucy." In his reply he wrote:

"Depend upon it, we know better than to repeal our Masculine systems."[24]

In the mid-19th century Susan B. Anthony, a woman's movement activist, said: "Marriage will never cease to be wholly an unequal partnership until the law recognizes equal ownership in the joint earnings and possessions."[25]

In 1915, Theodora W. Youmans, President of the Wisconsin Women's Suffrage Association, said:

> The assumption that women however hard they work in the household and however much of actual money value that work has, do not support themselves, but are supported by their husbands, that they earn nothing and own nothing—that assumption, upon which all property laws are based, is so abominable that I cannot find words to express my opinion of it.[26]

In the community property states, women's criticism of the property rights of spouses focused primarily on the wife's lack of a right to manage and control community property. Although husband and wife were equal owners of community property, the husband had the exclusive right to manage and control it during his lifetime. During the 1970s and 1980s, all of the eight community property states amended their property law to provide each spouse with equal rights to manage and control community property.

Property Rights of Married Women: A Recent National Concern

During the 1960s and 1970s the property rights of married women emerged as a national concern. Two presidents of the United States, John F. Kennedy and Gerald R. Ford, supported a national study of the rights of married women.

On December 14, 1961, President John F. Kennedy established by Executive Order the President's Commission on the Status of Women. He said:

. . . We have by no means done enough to strengthen family life and at the same time encourage women to make their full contribution as citizens. . . . It is appropriate at this time . . . to review recent accomplishments, and to acknowledge frankly the further steps that must be taken. This is a task for the entire nation.[27]

The Commission, composed of distinguished men and women, was directed to review the: "Differences in legal treatment of men and women in regard to political and civil rights, property rights, and family relations."[28]

The Commission reported in 1963, that ". . . in every state one kind of disability or another limits the legal rights of married women."[29] The Commission proposed that

> State legislatures and other groups concerned with the improvement of state statutes affecting family law and personal and property rights of married women . . . should move to eliminate laws that impose legal disabilities on women.[30]

The Commission specifically directed attention to these considerations:

> Marriage as a partnership in which each spouse makes a different but equally important contribution is increasingly recognized as a reality in this country. . . . During marriage each spouse should have a legally defined substantial right in the earnings of the other, in the real and personal property acquired with these earnings, and in their management. Such a right should be legally recognized as surviving the marriage in the event of its termination by divorce, annulment, or death. Appropriate legislation should safeguard either spouse and protect the surviving spouse against improper alienation of property by the other. . . .[31]

American Women, the report issued by the Commission in 1963, states:

> In making our proposals, we had in mind the well-being of the entire society; their adoption would in many cases be of direct benefit to men as well as women.[32]

On January 9, 1975, President Gerald R. Ford established by
Executive Order a National Commission on the Observance of
1975 as International Women's Year. The purpose of the Commission was to "promote equality between men and women."[33] The
Commission was authorized "to establish . . . subcommittees or
working groups as may be necessary for the fulfillment of its
tasks."[34]

The Homemaker Committee, one of 13 working groups, focused on federal and state tax laws, as well as the property rights
of married women.

One of the recommendations of the Commission was:

Full Partnership for the Homemaker: The goal of marriage as
a full partnership has not been achieved. The Commission asks
that the Nation's laws be based on the principle that a
homemaker's contribution is equal in value to the contribution of the spouse who works outside the home.[35]

. . . *To Form A More Perfect Union* . . . the report of the Commission issued in 1976, stated that the report was designed to im-
part "a sense of some of the barriers that keep women from participating in American life."[36]

Property Rights of Married Women: A Wisconsin Concern in the 1970s

Information gathered from married women who fulfilled the
traditional role of wife, mother, and full-time homemaker about
the inequities in the Wisconsin law governing the property rights
of spouses at conferences on "Homemaking and the Family:
Changing Values and Concerns" had an impact on the thinking
of many women in Wisconsin in leadership roles. *Real Women,
Real Lives, Marriage, Divorce, Widowhood*, published in 1978 by
the Governor's Commission on the Status of Women, docu-
mented the inequities in Wisconsin property law. The case histories, based on the experience of Wisconsin married women,
revealed the financial and economic hardships endured by married women and the legal consequences for both spouses. The

scope and magnitude of the inequities in the Wisconsin law governing the property rights of spouses made it clear that the need to reform the law governing the property rights of married women was urgent. Awareness of the inequities in the Wisconsin law governing the property rights of married women energized the legislative reform movement to redefine the legal rights of women in Wisconsin.

CHAPTER 5 ✺

Wisconsin's New Marital Property System, 1986 and After

The Wisconsin Legal Innovation

In the 1970s, some of the major issues shaping Wisconsin legislation were an Equal Rights Amendment to the Wisconsin Constitution, and ratification of the Equal Rights Amendment to the United States Constitution. Other issues of concern to the Wisconsin legislature were divorce reform, and the spousal inequities in the separate property system.

The Wisconsin legal innovation was the "Marital Partnership Property" reform proposal introduced in the Legislature in 1979. Later many principles of this creative proposal were incorporated into the Uniform Marital Property Act and culminated in the Wisconsin Marital Property Act enacted by the Legislature and signed by the Governor in 1984. This historic legislative achievement made Wisconsin the first state in the nation to change from a separate property system to a marital property system, a form of community property.

Necessity was the mother of invention. No model law existed in 1975 to guide the development of a legislative reform proposal to remedy the inequities in Wisconsin law governing the property rights of spouses in an ongoing marriage or at the death of a spouse. Hence, an Ad Hoc Committee, formed by the Governor's

Commission on the Status of Women, was asked to develop guidelines that would address these inequities.

The Ad Hoc Committee, composed of legislators, lawyers, law professors, University Extension staff, and representatives of citizen groups, approached its assignment in a systematic fashion. To meet the need for basic legal information, an already established clinical legal internship program at the Governor's Commission on the Status of Women was expanded. University of Wisconsin Law School students did the basic legal research for the Committee.

First, Wisconsin statutory law and case law governing the property rights of spouses were subjected to detailed examination. Various proposals to reform the separate property law were scrutinized by the Ad Hoc Committee. When it became apparent that incremental modifications of existing Wisconsin property law could not remove the underlying causes for the inequities in the property rights of spouses, alternative solutions were sought.

A variety of American and Canadian legal sources was explored as a basis for proposing alternative solutions. Each proposal was discussed and debated. As a result of these extensive intellectual exercises, members of the Ad Hoc Committee identified and selected the basic community property concepts essential for establishing equitable property right rules governing spouses. Organizing and synthesizing these legal concepts into one comprehensive statute that would govern the economic rights of spouses during marriage and their property rights at the death of a spouse presented a challenge.

Four years of research, decision making, and drafting led to the first legislative proposal, which was introduced in the legislature with bipartisan support as Assembly Bill 1090 on December 5, 1979 (also Senate Bill 474). The bill created a "Marital Partnership Property" system, and was based on community property principles. The initial strategy of the major authors was to get public reaction to the proposal and to invite feedback from all interested parties on how to revise and improve the proposal. The intent of this creative approach was to involve as many interested parties as possible in drafting an innovative legislative proposal that would establish equitable property rights for spouses and be a workable statute.

At the national level, a parallel effort was evolving. The National Conference of Commissioners on Uniform State Laws (NCCUSL) is not a legislative body. It is, in essence, a legal "think tank" that studies legal problems common to all 50 states, then develops and proposes draft state legislation to resolve a particular legal problem. If every state voluntarily adopts the proposed legislation, a uniform law nationwide is established.

In 1977, a special NCCUSL committee was appointed to study concurrent ownership of property and to determine if a uniform law on the subject was desirable. The committee reported that the most critical area was the property rights of married persons. It found that state laws governing the property rights of spouses differed considerably. In addition, many of the state laws were antiquated and were not responsive to current needs.

As a result of the report by the committee on concurrent ownership of property, the NCCUSL appointed a new committee in 1979 to draft a Uniform Marital Property Act. The drafting committee utilized the expertise and experience of the group working on marital property reform legislation in Wisconsin. In July, 1983, a Uniform Marital Property Act (proposing a community property system) was adopted by the National Conference of Commissioners on Uniform State Laws.

These two related national and Wisconsin efforts to develop a comprehensive marital property system based on community property principles culminated in Wisconsin legislation. Modified and refined versions of 1979 Assembly Bill 1090 were introduced in 1981 as Assembly Bill 370 (also Senate Bill 272), and in 1983 as Assembly Bill 200 (also Senate Bill 105). On September 23, 1983, the sponsors of the Wisconsin marital property reform legislation incorporated the Uniform Marital Property Act into 1983 Assembly Bill 200 with a limited number of modifications to meet certain Wisconsin situations. The basic principles and many of the provisions of the Uniform Marital Property Act and the Wisconsin bill were the same, so that this amalgamation was not difficult to draft. The uniform definitions and construction of the Uniform Marital Property Act were viewed by the sponsors of AB 200 as distinct advantages once the Uniform Act becomes adopted by other states. This strategic decision provided the momentum for the Wisconsin legislature to enact the comprehensive marital property reform legislation, rather than the less comprehensive alternative legislation sponsored by the State Bar of Wisconsin. The Governor signed the Marital Property Act on April 4, 1984. The law became effective January 1, 1986.

Marital Property System Characteristics

The Marital Property Act repealed Chapter 766 of the Wisconsin Statutes entitled "Property Rights of Married Women" and recreated Chapter 766 to read "Property Rights of Married Persons: Marital Property."

In Chapter 765 entitled "Marriage," marriage was redefined as a legal contract between two equal persons, husband and wife. In Chapter 766, the terms of the marriage contract were defined, and all remaining common law "disabilities of married women" were abolished.

The statute deals with the property rights of a married person, and identifies that person as a spouse; therefore the language of the law is gender neutral. The spouses have equal and identical rights. For the first time in Wisconsin, a written comprehensive law governs the property rights of married men and married women. One statute integrates the property rights of spouses in dealing with each other and with third parties. The Act governs the economic rights of spouses during an ongoing marriage and their property rights when that marriage ends with the death of a spouse. The law is prospective. In general, it applies only to property acquired by Wisconsin spouses on or after January 1, 1986.

The general legal principle underlying the marital property system is automatic sharing by spouses in property acquired during marriage. Marital property includes both income and property resulting from the personal efforts of either spouse during marriage. Both spouses own each and every item of marital property in equal, undivided shares. The ownership interest of each spouse is vested simultaneously upon the acquisition of income and property. Hence, ownership rights are created automatically by operation of law.

The philosophy on which the marital property system is based is that marriage creates an economic partnership for the well-being of the family. It is an economic unit in which the contributions made by each spouse in the form of services or money, or both, are of equal economic value. The law presumes that the income and property acquired during marriage are for the mutual benefit of the marital partnership.

Property classification, a key feature of the marital property system, is determined by two factors: 1) *when* the property was acquired (before or after marriage; before or after the "determination date"); 2) *what* the source of funds was (marital property or individual property).

"Determination date," as defined in the statute, is the date on which the provisions of the Marital Property Act affect the property rights of spouses living in Wisconsin. The "determination dates" are: 1) for married couples domiciled in Wisconsin before January 1, 1986, their "determination date" is January 1, 1986; 2) for persons in Wisconsin who marry on or after January 1, 1986, their "determination date" is the date of their marriage; 3) for married couples who move from another state to Wisconsin after December 31, 1985, their "determination date" is the date both spouses become domiciled in Wisconsin.

Only property acquired by either or both spouses after the Marital Property Act became effective on January 1, 1986, is classified as marital property or individual property. The Act is prospective and applies only to the future. The Act becomes effective for a married couple on their "determination date."

Property classification by statutory rules is a key characteristic of the marital property system. Statutory classification of property determines ownership. All property of a Wisconsin married couple acquired after their determination date is classified as either marital or individual. Property acquired during marriage and after the couple's determination date through the efforts of either or both spouses is marital property. Each spouse owns 50 percent of all marital property. Property owned before marriage and property acquired after marriage by gift or inheritance is individual property. The owner spouse is the sole owner of individual property.

Flexibility in the mandatory marital property system is provided through marital property agreements. Spouses have the freedom to modify most of the provisions of the marital property law by preparing and signing a written marital property agreement that fits their particular situation. A marital property agreement is enforceable in a court of law if it complies with the requirements of the Act. In 1988, amendments to the 1984 Marital Property Act created two special statutory forms of marital property agreements. One is a Statutory Terminable Marital Property Classification Agreement. The other is a Statutory Terminable Individual Property Classification Agreement.

Wisconsin is the first state in the nation to change from separate property law to marital property law, a form of community property. The Internal Revenue Service now recognizes Wisconsin as a community property state.

Major changes in the law governing the property rights of spouses in Wisconsin made by the Marital Property Act include: 1) property ownership; 2) property management and control; 3) access to credit; 4) obligations of spouses; 5) disposition of property at the death of a spouse; and 6) marital property agreements. Each major change in the law is explained in detail in the following sections of this chapter.

Marriage Redefined

The state legislature redefined marriage as a legal contract between two equal persons, husband and wife. In the Marital Property

Act, Chapter 765 of the Wisconsin Statutes, "Marriage" was amended to begin with this statement of legislative intent:

> . . . It is the intent of the legislature to recognize the valuable contributions of both spouses during marriage and at the termination of the marriage by dissolution or death. . . . between 2 equal persons, a husband and wife, who owe to each other mutual responsibility and support. Each spouse has an equal obligation in accordance with her or his ability to contribute money or services or both which are necessary for the adequate support and maintenance of her or his minor children and of the other spouse. No spouse may be presumed primarily liable for support expenses under this subsection. 765.001(2)

The new definition makes clear that marriage is a legal contract, and it also makes explicit what the marriage partners owe to each other. The original definition of marriage as a civil contract remains as a part of Chapter 765 of the Wisconsin Statutes.

Terms of Marriage Contract Defined

For the first time in Wisconsin the terms of the marriage contract are defined in one comprehensive chapter of the statutes. Chapter 766 of the Wisconsin Statutes, "Property Rights of Married Persons: Marital Property," governs the economic rights of spouses during an ongoing marriage and their property rights when that marriage ends with the death of a spouse.

Now everyone in Wisconsin has access to written law in a single statute that defines the terms of the marriage contract.

Common Law Disabilities of Married Women Abolished

All remaining English common law "disabilities of married women" were removed by statute in the 1984 Marital Property Act. Chapter 766 of the Wisconsin Statutes has two provisions that deal explicitly with common law "disabilities of married women." These are:

766.97(2) Nothing in this chapter revives the common law disabilities on a woman's right to own, manage, inherit, transfer or receive gifts of property in her own name, to enter into contracts in her own name or to institute civil actions in her own name. Except as otherwise provided in this chapter and in other sections of the statutes controlling marital property or individual property of spouses, either spouse has the right to own and exclusively manage his or her individual property, enter into contracts with 3rd parties or with his or her spouse, institute and defend civil actions in his or her name and maintain an action against his or her spouse for damages resulting from that spouse's intentional act or negligence.

766.97(3) The common law rights of a spouse to compel the domestic and sexual services of the other spouse are abolished. Nothing in this subsection affects a spouse's common law right to consortium or society and companionship.

Property Ownership

OVERVIEW

Classification of property by statutory definition determines ownership of property. There are two classifications: marital property and individual property. ("Unclassified" property is explained in Chapter 6.) Ownership determination by classification of property is a new concept in Wisconsin law. It applies to all forms of property acquired after December 31, 1985, by a married couple living in Wisconsin. If marital property and individual property are combined, the result is mixed property. Options to keep individual property classified as individual property are defined. New forms of holding property by document of title applicable *only* to husband and wife were created. A new form of an account at financial institutions available *only* to a married couple was created. If a married person owns property jointly with a third party, the nonowning spouse may have a marital property remedy as to that property. The spouses may act to reclassify their existing and future property if they choose to do so. Each of these aspects of the law governing the classification of property is addressed and explained.

MARITAL PROPERTY ACT PRESUMPTION

All property owned by spouses is presumed to be marital property unless another classification can be established.

The statutory presumption may be rebutted by sufficient evidence that funds used to acquire an asset were individual property. If documentation can be provided to trace the property back to its source of funds to establish that the property is *not* marital property, the property is classified as individual property.

The spouse who wants to assert individual ownership of any property is responsible for maintaining accurate records and the necessary documentation to establish its individual property classification.

MARITAL PROPERTY DEFINED

Generally, marital property consists of income and property resulting from the personal efforts of either spouse during marriage. By statutory definition marital property includes: 1) wages, salaries, and fringe benefits such as life insurance and pension plans resulting from paid employment of either or both husband and wife; 2) income or "fruits" such as dividends, interest, and net rents from both marital property and individual property; 3) assets acquired with marital property; 4) property designated as marital property by a marital property agreement, including a Statutory Terminable Marital Property Classification Agreement; and 5) property classified as marital property in a court decree.

Marital property is owned equally by both spouses. Each spouse has at present, undivided one-half interest in each and every item of marital property. Ownership rights of each spouse are vested simultaneously with the acquisition of income and property by operation of law.

Individual Property Defined

By statutory definition individual property includes: 1) property owned before marriage; 2) property acquired by one spouse after marriage by gift or inheritance from a third party or as an interspousal gift; 3) property received from a trust created by a third party; 4) property purchased with individual property; 5) income or "fruits" of property classified as individual property by a unilateral written statement signed by the spouse owning the asset (explained later); 6) property designated as individual property by a marital property agreement, including a Statutory Terminable Individual Property Classification Agreement (explained later); and 7) property designated as individual property by court decree.

Individual property of a spouse is owned solely by the owner spouse. If individual property is exchanged for other property or sold and the proceeds used to buy other property, the newly acquired property retains its original classification as individual property. However, if the name on the document of title to individual property is changed as a result of the transaction, a reclassification of that property has probably occurred.

Mixed Property

Mixed property has both a marital property component and an individual property component. Mixed property may be created in a variety of ways.

One example: A spouse has a savings account which was started with inherited money (individual property). The interest earned or paid on or after their determination date is marital property under the new law. If the interest is added to the principal to earn compound interest, the result is mixed property, unless a spouse has executed a unilateral statement (explained later).

Another example: An unmarried person bought a house and made the down payment and mortgage payments with solely owned property (individual property). After the couple's determination date, the mortgage payments were made with marital property. The result is mixed property.

A less familiar way of creating mixed property is by renovating or remodeling individual property such as a historic house, heirloom furniture, or antique car, that results in a substantial increase in the value of the individual property. If substantial efforts of either spouse were made without reasonable compensation, any resulting substantial increase in the value of the individual property after the couple's determination date is classified as marital property.

A mixed property asset will be reclassified as all marital property if adequate records are not available to trace the individual property component. The spouse who wants to assert ownership of her/his individual property must assume the responsibility for proving its individual property classification. Tracing individual property back to its source can be done if the owner spouse has the appropriate legal evidence. The kinds of evidence needed to establish individual classification of property include: 1) accurate records of property acquired by gift or inheritance, of investments made from earnings prior to marriage, and of property acquired through sale or purchase of individual property assets; 2) documents showing transfer of title to property, cancelled checks, receipts, and other proofs of purchase.

LIFE INSURANCE

Special rules apply to life insurance policies for several reasons. One is their importance to many couples as a valuable economic asset. Another is that they are typically purchased on an installment basis, in which some payments may predate and some postdate the determination date of the couple. Still another is the desirability of a uniform statutory rule.

How much of the proceeds of the decedent's life insurance policy is marital property depends upon the existence of a marital property component in the policy. If a life insurance policy is issued after the determination date to a married person as the insured and the insured spouse is the owner of the policy (the typical situation, and the insured owner has the right to designate the beneficiary), the policy is classified as marital property regardless of whether the premiums are paid with marital or individual property.

If a life insurance policy is issued to a single person prior to marriage, the policy is property brought to the marriage, and therefore the property of that person. However when that person marries, as soon as one premium is paid with marital property either by the spouse or by the employer of the spouse, a marital property portion is created, and the policy is treated as mixed property. The new classification of a portion of the policy as marital property is permanent and is applicable thereafter, even if all later premiums are paid with individual property.

If a life insurance policy classified as mixed property has a marital property portion and an individual property portion at the death of the insured spouse, a statutory formula determines what portion of the policy is marital property and what portion is individual property. The surviving spouse has a right to one-half of the proceeds classified as that spouse's marital property interest, regardless of the named beneficiary. The designated beneficiary is entitled to the remainder of the proceeds.

If the life insurance policy of a spouse has a third party (someone other than a spouse) as the named beneficiary, the named beneficiary owns all of the proceeds *only* if the noninsured spouse has released or waived her/his marital property interest in the proceeds. Even if the named beneficiary is the parent or child of either spouse, a written release or waiver by the noninsured spouse is required.

The noninsured spouse may release or reclassify the marital property interest in the proceeds or premiums of a life insurance policy by: 1) a marital property agreement (explained later); or 2) a written consent statement. A written consent statement may be revoked later unless the original statement expressly states it may not be revoked. The statement must be drafted carefully to avoid adverse gift tax consequences for the spouse signing the consent statement.

There is a different classification rule for a life insurance policy where the spouse of the insured is the owner. The ownership interest and proceeds of such a life insurance policy are classified as the individual property of the owner regardless of whether marital or individual property is used to pay the premiums. (This rule covers only situations where the spouse of the insured is *owner* of the policy, *not* the beneficiary.)

DEFERRED EMPLOYMENT BENEFIT PLAN

A special rule applies to a deferred employment benefit plan. To protect the employee spouse if the nonemployee spouse dies first, a policy decision was made to deviate from the general marital property concepts for the deferred employment benefit plan. The Marital Property Act gives a broad definition to such plans, and states:

> [A] "deferred employment benefit plan" means a plan, fund, program, or other arrangement under which compensation or other benefits from employment are expressly, or as a result of surrounding circumstances, deferred to a later date or the happening of a future event. "Deferred employment benefit plan" includes but is not limited to a pension, profit sharing, or stock-bonus plan, and an employee stock-ownership or stock-purchase plan, a savings or thrift plan, an annuity plan, a qualified bond purchase plan, a self-employed retirement plan, a simplified employee pension, and a deferred compensation agreement or plan.

If new employment of a spouse after the couple's determination date results in a deferred employment benefit plan for the employee spouse, the entire plan is classified as marital property.

If an employee spouse receives a sum of money as a part of a deferred employment benefit plan and the money is rolled over into an Individual Retirement Account, that portion of the IRA is recognized as a deferred employment benefit. Any other IRA financed out of current income is classified as marital property, and is not covered by the special rules for deferred retirement benefit plans.

The nonemployee spouse has a marital property interest in a deferred employee benefit plan of the employee spouse. This means that at the death of the employee spouse a surviving non-employee spouse has a right to claim her/his marital property interest in the benefit plan. If the nonemployee spouse dies before the employee spouse, however, there is a special rule stating that the marital property interest of the nonemployee spouse terminates. Thus, the surviving employee spouse retains full rights to the plan's benefits. Also, if the nonemployee spouse predeceases the employee spouse, the marital property interest of the nonemployee spouse in an Individual Retirement Account traceable to a deferred employment benefit plan terminates with the death of the nonemployee spouse.

Federal rules govern the property rights of spouses in many private deferred employment benefit plans, and may preempt the Wisconsin Marital Property Act rules. The Federal Employee Retirement Income Security Act (ERISA) was amended by the Federal Retirement Equity Act of 1984 (REA). The REA amendments deal with pre-retirement and post-retirement benefits. One amendment provides that 50 percent of the pre-retirement death benefits covered by law must be paid to the surviving spouse of a pension plan participant regardless of the designated beneficiary at the time of death, unless the surviving spouse has consented in writing to another designated beneficiary.

The other amendment covers post-retirement benefits. A pension plan that provides retirement benefits to a married person must provide for a husband and wife pension or a joint and survivor benefit. The income from the pension must cover the lives of the employee and the employee's spouse unless written consent to choose another plan has been given by the spouse of the employee. The federal legislation specifies the required consent form.

BUSINESS OWNERSHIP

If a spouse acquires a business (as sole proprietor, as a partnership, or as a stockholder in a closely held corporation) after the couple's determination date with individual property, the business is classified as individual property of the owner spouse. In that case, the other spouse has no ownership right in the business.

However, the business may become mixed property with a marital property component. Even if the owner spouse does not actively participate in the business, the income generated by the business is by statutory definition marital property, unless the owner spouse has executed a unilateral statement. Also, if either spouse works in the business classified as individual property of one spouse, the income earned by either or both is marital property. If they reinvest their income in the business, it becomes mixed property with a marital property component. Each spouse has a marital property interest in the marital property component, but the individual property component is owned exclusively by the owner spouse. The spouse who acquired the business has sole management and control, even if there is a marital property component.

The owner spouse who wants to preserve and maintain the individual property classification of the business has the sole and exclusive responsibility for documenting its individual property classification back to the original source of funds. If the owner spouse cannot trace and establish the individual property classification of a component, the entire business is reclassified as marital property.

A substantial increase in the value of an individual property business may affect the property rights of the spouses. "Active" appreciation may create a marital property component in the business, while "passive" appreciation does not.

In this context, "Active" appreciation means a substantial increase in the value of the business due to a substantial effort of one or both spouses. If reasonable compensation is not received by the spouse for the substantial effort expended, a marital property component is created, and the nonowner spouse has a marital property interest in that component of the business. If reasonable compensation is received by the spouse whose substantial effort resulted in the increased value of the business, no marital property component is created, and the "active" appreciation in the value of the business is individual property.

"Passive" appreciation means a substantial increase in the value of the business due to external forces such as inflationary or market forces, without any effort of the owner or the nonowner spouse. Such an increase in individual property after the couple's determination date is considered "passive" appreciation and remains the individual property of the owner spouse.

NEW FORMS OF HOLDING PROPERTY JOINTLY BY DOCUMENT OF TITLE

The 1984 Marital Property Act created two new forms of holding property by document of title exclusively for husband and wife. One is marital property. The other is survivorship marital property.

Property held by husband and wife by document of title as marital property means each spouse has an undivided, equal ownership interest in the property and has the right to will one-half the marital property at death. In the absence of a valid will the decedent's one-half interest in marital property passes under the laws of intestacy.

Property held by husband and wife by document of title as survivorship marital property means each spouse has an undivided, equal ownership interest in the property, and neither spouse can will any part of such property. At the death of a spouse the entire property becomes the property of the surviving spouse by operation of law. Survivorship marital property is not subject to the laws of intestacy. However, a surviving spouse may disclaim the decedent spouse's interest in survivorship marital property under Wisconsin law relating to disclaimers of transfers under nontestamentary instruments. The disclaimer provision may be useful to some couples as part of their post-mortem estate planning.

Property held by document of title as marital property or as survivorship marital property has certain tax advantages that are explained later.

A married couple may continue to use a "tenants-in-common" or a "joint tenancy" form of owning property. However, if a married couple creates by document of title a "tenants-in-common" form of ownership exclusively between husband and wife after their determination date, the property is classified as marital property. If a married couple creates by document of title a "joint tenant" form of property ownership exclusively between husband and wife after their determination date, the property is classified as survivorship marital property.

If the Marital Property Act does not apply to spouses when property is acquired on or after January 1, 1986, because only one spouse is domiciled in Wisconsin or neither spouse is yet domiciled in Wisconsin, the current Wisconsin law applies. It provides that if the owners, transferees, or buyers are described in a document of title, an instrument of transfer or bill of sale as husband and wife, or are in fact husband and wife, they are "joint tenants," unless the intent to create a "tenancy-in-common" is expressed.

HOMESTEAD OWNERSHIP

Special classification rules govern a homestead acquired by husband and wife after December 31, 1985. If the real estate is to be the primary personal residence of the married couple upon purchase and is "titled" at the time of acquisition in the names of both husband and wife (but no third party), and there is no indication of a different intent in the deed or document of title, the homestead property is classified as survivorship marital property. The classification rule means that at the death of the first spouse, the surviving spouse automatically owns the entire asset, and the property passes by operation of law without probate.

This special classification rule does *not* apply if the homestead deed or document of title states the property is owned, by husband and wife, as marital property or as "tenants-in-common." There is no survivorship right in property held by document of title as marital property.

A homestead, like any other property, may be reclassified at any time by a variety of methods, including a marital property agreement.

A New Financial Account: the Marital Account

The 1984 Marital Property Act created a new type of financial institution account called a marital account. *Only* a couple claiming to be husband and wife can establish a marital account after December 31, 1985, in any financial institution in Wisconsin. Financial institutions are commercial banks, trust companies, savings banks, building and loan associations, savings and loan associations, and credit unions.

Generally, a marital account is an account without the right of survivorship. During the lifetime of both husband and wife either spouse may withdraw some or all of the funds. At the death of a spouse the surviving spouse owns one-half of the sums on deposit, and the decedent's estate owns the other half. However, if the decedent spouse named one or more payable-on-death (POD) beneficiaries to receive her/his one-half interest in the marital account, the property passes to the designated beneficiaries by operation of law without probate. If no P. O. D beneficiaries were named by the decedent, the decedent's one-half of the marital account passes under the will, or in the absence of a valid will, passes under the laws of intestacy.

The Joint Account

In contrast to a marital account, a joint account in a financial institution may be established by two or more persons and has the right of survivorship. For instance, a joint bank account may be established by a mother and son, a father and daughter, or three unrelated persons who wish to use a joint bank account to pay shared living expenses. A husband and wife may establish a joint account as well as a marital account.

During the lifetime of the parties any one of the parties to the joint account may withdraw some or all of the funds on deposit. At the death of one of the parties, the surviving party or parties become the owners of the entire account, and the property passes by operation of law without probate.

Property Held by a Married Person and a Third Party

A married person may hold property by document of title with a third person in three different ways: 1) as "tenants-in-common"; 2) as "joint tenants"; 3) as co-owners of a joint account in a financial institution. In each case the marital property interest of the nonparty spouse is protected.

If a married person creates a "tenants-in-common" form of property ownership with a third party by document of title after that married person's determination date, a marital property component may exist. The Marital Property Act does not change the ownership rights of parties to a "tenants-in-common" form of ownership. However, if the married person made a gift of marital property either in the form of money or substantial labor to the co-owner without the consent of the nonparty spouse, the nonparty spouse has a marital property interest in the property that is recognized by law. At the death of the married person the nonparty spouse has a marital property interest in the decedent's "tenancy-in-common" interest in the property.

If a married person creates a "joint tenancy" form of property ownership with a third party by document of title after the married person's determination date, a marital property remedy may exist. The Marital Property Act did not change the right of survivorship of any "joint tenancy" form of property ownership. However, if the married person made a gift of marital property either in the form of money or substantial effort to the co-owner without the consent of the spouse who was not a party to the "joint tenancy," at the death of the married person the nonparty spouse to the "joint tenancy" has a special remedy available. The nonparty spouse is entitled to reimbursement from the decedent's estate or from the third party, based upon the value of what would have been a marital property component.

If a married person creates a joint account with a third party in a financial institution after December 31, 1985, and deposits marital property into the account without the consent of the nonparty spouse, the nonparty spouse has a gift remedy available. At the death of the donor spouse when the transfer of property becomes a completed gift, the nonparty spouse may recover her/his marital property interest in the marital property component of the joint account from the third party. The surviving spouse may, also, have the right to trace withdrawals made by the deceased spouse, and claim a marital property interest in other assets acquired with funds from this account.

RECLASSIFICATION OF PROPERTY

Reclassification of property may sometimes be done independently by one spouse or by both spouses acting together. One spouse may independently reclassify property by: 1) making a gift of marital property to a third party or to his or her spouse; or by executing a written consent statement to release her/his marital property interest in the proceeds or premiums of a life insurance policy; 2) executing a unilateral written statement to reclassify income or "fruits" of individual property from marital property to individual property.

A unilateral written statement (a document made without permission or agreement of the nonowning spouse) may be made by the owner spouse to change the classification of post-determination date income or "fruits" of individual property from marital property to individual property. To reclassify the income from individual property, the owner spouse must: 1) declare in writing that the income or "fruits" of some or all of her/his individual property is individual property and sign the statement; 2) have the statement acknowledged by a notary public; 3) give notice of the statement to the nonowning spouse. Within five days of execution, the notice must be personally delivered to the nonowning spouse, or be sent by certified mail to the last known address.

A person intending to marry may execute a unilateral written statement (a document made without permission or agreement of the other marriage partner) classifying the income attributable to her or his property other than marital property as individual property. A statement executed by a person intending to marry is effective upon the marriage, or at a later time if so provided in the statement. Within five days after the statement is executed, the person executing the statement must notify the person she or he intends to marry or has married, of the statement's contents by personally delivering a copy of the statement to that person or by sending a copy by certified mail. Failure to give such notice is a breach of the duty of good faith under the Marital Property Act.

The unilateral statement is prospective; it applies only to the future. Only the income or "fruits" earned or paid after the effective date of the unilateral statement will be reclassified as individual property. To reclassify income or "fruits" received before the effective date of the unilateral statement, a marital property agreement may be used.

The right to reclassify unilaterally unearned income or "fruits" of individual property (interest, dividends, net rent) does *not* apply to earned income (wages, salary, profits) which by statutory definition is marital property, and may be reclassified only by agreement or gift.

Both spouses together may reclassify property by: 1) signing a deed transferring real estate; 2) signing an instrument transferring securities; 3) signing a marital property agreement, including a statutory terminable marital property classification agreement form and a statutory terminable individual property classification agreement form. Each of these methods of reclassifying property requires the signatures of both spouses. However, the statutory agreement forms require that the signature of each spouse must be authenticated by a Wisconsin lawyer or acknowledged before a Wisconsin notary public. (A marital property agreement and the statutory property classification agreement forms are explained in a later section.)

EXCEPTIONS TO STATUTORY CLASSIFICATION OF PROPERTY AS MARITAL PROPERTY

The Marital Property Act provides for certain exceptions to the statutory classification of property as marital property. Income from two specified sources is exempt. A life insurance policy under specified circumstances is also exempt.

Income from individual property that is exempt from classification as marital property, and is classified as individual property is: 1) income from a trust created by a third party for the benefit of one spouse unless the trust provides otherwise; 2) income from a gift from one spouse to the other spouse, unless a contrary intent of the donor spouse is established.

A life insurance policy with a designated owner or a designated beneficiary acquired under a court judgment or a property settlement agreement incident to a prior marriage or to parenthood is *not* marital property regardless of whether marital property or individual property is used to pay the premiums.

Management and Control of Marital Property

OVERVIEW

Generally, management and control rights of marital property are determined by the names of the spouses on the document of title to marital property. Under the marital property system, a name on a document of title does *not* determine ownership of property, although it does determine many management and control rights. This is a new concept in Wisconsin law. The form used on the document of title determines when one spouse may act alone and when both spouses must act together. The broadly defined management and control rights of spouses include: 1) gifts of marital property to third parties; 2) sale of marital property; and 3) buy-sell agreements. Safeguards to protect the marital property interest of the nonmanaging spouse are also provided.

DOCUMENT OF TITLE FORMS

The form of the document of title to marital property determines a spouse's right to manage and control that property. There are three forms of holding title to marital property.

If the marital property is held by document of title in the name of one spouse only, that marital property is managed solely by the named spouse.

If the marital property is held by document of title in the names of both spouses joined by the word "or" (name of one spouse *or* name of other spouse), either spouse may manage all of that marital property.

If the marital property is held by document of title in the names of both spouses joined by the word "and" (name of husband *and* name of wife), both spouses must act together in managing that marital property.

How property is "held" is evidenced generally by a document of title such as a deed to real estate, a certificate of deposit, a corporate stock certificate, a certificate of title to a car, or a writing that customarily serves as a document of title. However, since there is nothing that customarily serves as a document of title for "uncertificated securities" (a security not represented by an instrument issued in bearer or registered form) and the property rights of a partner in a general partnership, the definition of "held" was expanded to include: 1) an "uncertificated security" is held by the person identified as the registered owner of the security upon the books maintained for that purpose by or on behalf of the issuer of the security; and 2) the property rights of a partner in a general partnership are held by the partner. This expanded definition of "held," authorized by the 1988 amendment to the Marital Property Act, gives the exclusive right to manage and control the "uncertificated security" and a general partnership right to the holding spouse.

Management and Control Rights Defined

The right to manage and control marital property is broadly defined and inclusive. The statutory definition is:

> 766.01(11) "Management and control" means the right to buy, sell, use, transfer, exchange, abandon, lease, consume, expend, assign, create a security interest in, mortgage, encumber, dispose of, institute or defend a civil action regarding or otherwise deal with property as if it were property of an unmarried person.

Marital Property Gifts to Third Parties

Either spouse may make gifts of marital property, which he or she has the right to manage, to third parties. However, the size of the gift made by the managing spouse acting alone is limited. Failure to observe the limit set by law provides the other spouse with a remedy.

The managing spouse acting alone has the right to make certain unilateral (without consent of the nonmanaging spouse) gifts to third parties. Unilateral gifts are limited to $1,000 per recipient or per person or entity in a calendar year unless a larger amount is "reasonable considering the economic position of the spouses." Third parties include relatives (children, parents), non-relatives, and charities.

Gifts exceeding the "safe harbor" limit of $1,000 per year, per donee (assuming the couples' economic position does not justify a larger amount) require the consent of the nonmanaging spouse either at the time the gift is made or later. If the managing spouse fails to obtain consent of the nonmanaging spouse on gifts larger than the legal limit, the nonmanaging spouse has the right to recover the property or the amount of the gift in excess of $1,000 from either the recipient or the managing spouse.

Sale of Marital Property

The Marital Property Act protects third parties (someone other than a spouse) who buy marital property from a managing spouse acting alone. If marital property is purchased from a spouse having the right to manage and control that property, and is acquired by a "bona fide purchaser," then the buyer is free from the claims of the nonmanaging spouse. This rule governing the sale of marital property cannot be varied by a marital property agreement.

The term "bona fide purchaser" is broadly defined in the Act as a person acting in good faith who acquires an interest in marital property by means other than a gift.

Buy-sell Agreements

The Marital Property Act protects third parties who enter into a buy-sell agreement with the managing spouse acting alone.

If the spouse having management and control of the marital property is a party to the agreement, the buy-sell agreement and any other executory contract (one which depends upon a future performance or event) for the sale of property protects the third party regardless of whether the agreement or contract is entered into before or after the spouse's determination date. The rights of the other spouse or any person acquiring an interest in the property are subject to the terms of the buy-sell agreement or executory contract.

Nonmanaging Spouse's Marital Property Interest Protected

The Marital Property Act protects the marital property interest of the nonmanaging spouse from abuse when the managing spouse acts alone in the management and control of marital property.

The chief protection of the nonmanaging spouse is the requirement that each spouse act in "good faith" with respect to the other spouse in matters involving marital property. If there is a lack of "good faith" in managing marital property or gross mismanagement or waste to the financial detriment of the other spouse, the law provides the nonmanaging spouse with several court remedies.

Spousal remedies are designed to: 1) prevent further financial damage to the marital property interest of the nonmanaging spouse; and 2) compensate for the financial damage already done to the marital property interest of the nonmanaging spouse.

To prevent further financial damage to the marital property the nonmanaging spouse has the right to ask the court to: 1) order the addition of her/his name to the document of title of marital property such as financial accounts, deeds to real estate, publicly traded stock certificates except certain business property; 2) order an accounting of the spouses' property and obligations if not done voluntarily by the managing spouse; 3) settle a disagreement over the classification of property (unless the spouses have agreed to arbitrate the disagreement); 4) limit or terminate the management and control rights of the managing spouse if she/he becomes incompetent or otherwise unable to manage the marital property; and 5) order certain actions such as naming one spouse as the sole manager of marital property, dividing the responsibility for existing obligations, assigning further obligations to the incurring spouse, classifying property as individual property of the acquiring spouse if substantial harm to marital property is due to the managing spouse's absence, mismanagement, or waste.

Compensation for financial damage already done to the marital property interest of the nonmanaging spouse can be obtained by the nonmanaging spouse in these ways: 1) she/he has a statutory claim against the managing spouse for compensation equal to the financial damage incurred if the managing spouse fails to act in "good faith" in the management of marital property in the best interests of both spouses; 2) she/he may bring a court action against the managing spouse, the recipient of the gift, or both to recover the property or any amount over the legal gift limit if the managing spouse made gifts to third parties in excess of that limit without the consent of the other spouse; 3) she/he may bring a court action for remedies to unconsented gifts that are not effective or completed until the death of the managing spouse, such as a gift of marital property in the form of a "joint tenancy"; and 4) she/he (the nondebtor spouse) has the right to ask the court for reimbursement by reclassifying an equal amount of marital property as her/his individual property if the managing spouse used marital property to satisfy a nonmarital debt.

Credit and Obligations

Overview

Credit and obligations of a married couple are linked together in the marital property system. Access to specified types of credit by an applicant spouse is based on a key exception to the general rule governing management and control of marital property. To satisfy the obligations of spouses, the property that may be reached by creditors is specified.

Creditors have certain rights and responsibilities. The applicant spouse has certain responsibilities. The nonapplicant spouse has certain rights. Federal and state regulations governing a spouse's access to credit carry penalties if not observed.

The Marital Property Act integrates a system for classifying obligations of spouses with a system for specifying the property that creditors may reach to satisfy an obligation. The liability of spousal property for debts incurred by the other spouse during marriage and at the death of a spouse is defined.

Credit Access

Creditworthiness (financial ability and willingness to pay creditors) determines a spouse's access to credit. Under the Marital Property Act the creditworthiness of the applicant spouse is established by the special 100 percent rule: either spouse acting alone may manage and control all marital property (100 percent) for specified types of credit as a marital obligation. The 100 percent rule is an exception to the general rule governing the management and control of marital property.

The special 100 percent rule governing management and control of marital property does *not* apply to certain business property interests: 1) interests in a partnership or joint venture held by the other spouse as a general partner or as a participant; 2) interests in professional corporations or associations held by the other spouse as a stockholder or member; 3) assets of an unincorporated business if the other spouse is the only spouse involved in operating or managing the business; and 4) interest in a corporation the stock of which is not publicly traded, if the other spouse is an employee of the corporation.

Types of Credit Specified

The specified types of credit covered by the special 100 percent rule governing the management and control of marital property are: 1) unsecured credit; 2) secured credit where the collateral or security is the item purchased.

Unsecured credit typically involves: 1) charge accounts at retail and service establishments; 2) credit cards acceptable by a variety of business firms. With open-end unsecured credit the creditor permits the consumer to make purchases or obtain cash advances from time to time, and the debtor promises to pay the creditor upon presentation of the bill the amount owed—either the full amount that is due or a minimum amount with interest on the unpaid balance. The creditor has no special legal right to repossess the items purchased.

Secured credit refers to purchases where there is a general promise to pay, and the item purchased is the collateral or security for the credit such as cars and household appliances. The creditor has the right to repossess the purchased item as well as sue for any unpaid balance if the debtor fails to make the scheduled payments. The legal procedure for repossession and the rights of the debtor (buyer) as well as the rights of the creditor (seller) are defined in the Wisconsin Consumer Act.

Secured credit transactions generally are not affected by the special 100 percent rule. A secured credit transaction is one in which the credit applicant owns the collateral (corporate stock, government bonds, real estate) and pledges the collateral as security for the credit requested, such as a loan. The only exception for secured credit transactions in which the special 100 percent rule applies is the secured credit where the collateral or security is the item purchased, such as a car.

TYPE OF OBLIGATION SPECIFIED

A family purpose obligation is the only type of obligation covered by the special 100 percent rule governing the management and control of marital property. A family purpose obligation is defined as a voluntary debt incurred by a spouse in the interest of the marriage or family. The Marital Property Act presumes that an obligation incurred by a spouse during marriage is in the interest of the marriage or family. If a spouse signs a statement that the obligation is in the interest of the marriage or family, the statement permits the creditor to classify the debt with certainty. (This statement, while conclusive evidence for the creditor as to the classification of the debt, does not affect any interspousal remedy which is available to the other spouse.)

CREDITOR RIGHTS AND RESPONSIBILITIES

Creditors have several rights and responsibilities. One is the right of the creditor to inquire about the marital status of the applicant. Marital and individual property rights and existing spousal obligations are relevant to any credit transaction of a married person.

The creditor has the responsibility of giving notice on every credit application for transactions governed by the Wisconsin Consumer Act if the creditor is to be bound by the provisions of the credit applicant's marital property agreement. If the creditor extends credit after receiving the marital property agreement, the creditor is bound by the terms of any property classification, characterization of an obligation, or management and control right described by the document.

The creditor also has the responsibility for giving written notice to the nonapplicant spouse if the creditor extends credit for transactions covered by the Wisconsin Consumer Act (most consumer transactions), and the credit may result in a family purpose obligation. The creditor is required to give this written notice to the nonapplicant spouse before any payment is due, unless the nonapplicant spouse had actual knowledge of the credit or waived notice in writing. The Marital Property Act provides penalties for creditors who fail to give the required written notice.

The rights and remedies of a married person who incurs a family purpose obligation covered by the Wisconsin Consumer Act are the same for both spouses. These provisions of the Wisconsin Consumer Act apply to family purpose credit transactions governed by the Marital Property Act.

Credit Applicant Responsibilities

The applicant spouse or debtor has the responsibility for furnishing the creditor with a copy of any marital property agreement governing credit transactions at the time of application for credit, if the creditor is to be bound by the property classification, characterization of an obligation, or management and control rights of spouses contained in the agreement. The creditor's rights cannot be adversely affected by a marital property agreement if the creditor does not have knowledge of the applicable provisions of the agreement or does not receive a copy of the marital property agreement prior to granting credit.

The applicant spouse or debtor has the responsibility for furnishing the creditor with a copy of a unilateral statement reclassifying the income or "fruits" of individual property at the time of application for credit if the creditor is to be bound by the unilateral statement. The creditor's rights cannot be adversely affected by a unilateral statement reclassifying the income or "fruits" of individual property if the creditor did not have knowledge of the contents of the statement or receive a copy of the statement prior to granting credit.

Rights of Nonapplicant Spouse

The nonapplicant spouse has the right to terminate liability for future extensions of credit by giving the creditor a written notice terminating her/his liability for the credit account.

REGULATION OF INDEPENDENT ACCESS TO CREDIT

Federal and state regulations govern an applicant spouse's access to credit in addition to the provisions of the Marital Property Act.

The Federal Equal Credit Opportunity Act specifies situations in a community property state where a creditor may *not* require the signature of the nonapplicant spouse.

Under the Marital Property Act, Wisconsin requires creditors to evaluate property of married persons in the same manner as the property of unmarried persons in determining the creditworthiness of a person applying for family purpose credit.

Violation of these provisions by creditors is subject to penalties under both federal and state laws.

VOLUNTARY OBLIGATIONS OF SPOUSES

The Marital Property Act integrates a system which classifies the voluntary obligations or debts of spouses with a system which specifies the property that can be reached by creditors to satisfy spousal debts.

The system that classifies voluntary obligations or debts of spouses is based on: 1) the purpose of the debt (family purpose, support obligation, nonmarital obligation); 2) the identity of the spouse responsible for the debt (obligated or nonobligated spouse; incurring or nonincurring spouse); 3) when the debt was incurred (pre-marriage, pre-Act, pre-determination date, post-determination date).

The system that specifies the property a creditor can reach to satisfy a voluntary obligation or debt is based on: 1) the kind of spousal property (marital, individual); 2) the amount of marital property (100 percent, or 50 percent); 3) the order in which different kinds of spousal property must be reached by creditors for a tort obligation.

A family purpose obligation may be satisfied from *all* of the marital property (100 percent) and all other property of the incurring spouse in whichever order the creditor chooses. If one spouse incurs a family purpose obligation, the income of both spouses (marital property) is available to satisfy the debt. For family purpose obligations, creditors can reach *all* of the marital property (100 percent) because creditors are required to consider *all* of the marital property (100 percent) in determining the creditworthiness of an applicant spouse acting alone, and because a family purpose obligation is presumed to benefit the marriage or family. Creditors' access to *all* of the marital property (100 percent) counterbalances spousal rights to obtain credit and emphasizes spousal responsibility to pay for marital debts.

Debts incurred by one spouse alone before January 1, 1986, are classified as pre-Act or pre-determination date obligations of that spouse. Creditors can reach only the nonmarital property of the incurring spouse and that part of the marital property that would have been the sole property of the incurring spouse except for the Marital Property Act (particularly wages or salary). This means that creditors cannot reach more property under the new law than they could reach previously to satisfy a debt.

Support of a child or support of a spouse from a prior marriage is considered a voluntary obligation incurred by a spouse before the present marriage. Hence, it is a pre-marriage obligation of the obligated spouse. It may be satisfied from the nonmarital property of the obligated spouse and from that part of the marital property which, except for marriage and the new property law, would be the sole property of the obligated spouse (wages or salary). None of the nonobligated spouse's wages or salary is available to satisfy such a debt.

The Marital Property Act does not alter the relationship between spouses and their creditors with respect to any property or obligation in existence on the couple's determination date. Furthermore, if one spouse is not domiciled in Wisconsin, the nonobligated spouse is not liable for an obligation of the incurring spouse.

Tort Obligation of a Spouse

A special rule applies to a tort obligation incurred by a spouse during marriage. A tort is a negligent or intentional act, such as a collision of a car driven by a spouse with another automobile which may result in liability. The damage resulting from a tort may be a tort obligation. An obligation resulting from a tort committed by a spouse during marriage may be satisfied from nonmarital property of the incurring spouse and from that spouse's interest in marital property.

LIABILITY OF ONE SPOUSE FOR DEBTS INCURRED BY OTHER SPOUSE AND FOR DEBTS OF A DECEASED SPOUSE

During marriage a spouse may limit the extent to which her/his property is liable for the debts incurred by the other spouse by: 1) entering into a marital property agreement with the other spouse with a provision addressing this issue; and/or 2) by maintaining good records and documentation for tracing a spouse's individual property.

Attachment of a judgment lien to real property of a nonobligated spouse or former spouse of a judgment debtor acquired *after* the judgment is docketed may occur because there is no practical mechanism to automatically exclude such property from attachment. Real property of a nonobligated spouse or former spouse of a judgment debtor acquired *after* the judgment is docketed is not available to satisfy the underlying obligation because it is exempt from a judgment lien.

In circumstances where a judgment lien does in fact attach to property not available to satisfy the underlying obligation, specific procedures to lift the lien judgment from such property were provided by an amendment to the Marital Property Act. One procedure applies *before* execution is issued in connection with the enforcement of a judgment lien. A second procedure is provided to apply *after* execution is issued. The procedures permit declaratory relief if a recordable release of the property from the judgment lien is not obtained. The second procedure prevents the property from being sold in connection with the enforcement of the judgment lien while the release or declaratory judgment is sought.

Liability of the surviving spouse for debts of a deceased spouse are treated according to the type of debt. For one type of debt, property that would have been available to creditors during the decedent's lifetime is available to creditors at the decedent's death for debts incurred by the deceased spouse, with certain exceptions. Some of these exceptions are: 1) survivorship marital property; 2) certain joint tenancy property subject to a judgment lien; 3) the decedent's deferred employment benefits; 4) property exempt from the claims of creditors against a decedent's estate as provided by statute. For the other kind of debt that involves a debt to a creditor who does not regularly extend credit such as personal loans, a gambling debt, the liability of the surviving spouse is limited. The income of the surviving spouse is not available for the satisfaction of this type of debt. The marital property assets of the surviving spouse are available only to the extent of their value on the date of the decedent's death.

If a marital property agreement governs the disposition of property at the death of a spouse, it does not affect the property available to a creditor to satisfy an obligation of a spouse, unless under the agreement that property was not available to the creditor while both spouses were alive.

Individual property owned by one spouse cannot be reached by creditors for the satisfaction of any obligation or debt incurred by the other spouse, unless the obligation is considered to be an obligation based upon the other spouse's duty to support.

Disposition of Property at Death of a Spouse

OVERVIEW

The Marital Property Act affects: 1) the amount of property each spouse has the right to dispose of at death; 2) the surviving spouse's rights in the decedent's probate and nonprobate estate; 3) the laws of intestacy; 4) the responsibilities and rights of the Personal Representative; 5) the powers of a guardian of an incompetent spouse; 6) the procedures for informal administration of an estate; 7) the economic protections of the surviving spouse; 8) the tax advantages of marital property at or after death of a spouse.

AMOUNT OF PROPERTY EACH SPOUSE HAS THE RIGHT TO DISPOSE OF AT DEATH

Under the marital property system each spouse (husband or wife) generally has the right to dispose of one-half of all property acquired during marriage because each spouse owns one-half of each and every item of marital property, even if the name of only one spouse is on the document of title to marital property. Each spouse also has the right to dispose of all of her/his individual property acquired by gift or inheritance as well as property owned before marriage. The method of disposing of each spouse's property interests is a matter of choice. Each spouse has a right to select the methods appropriate to achieve her/his objectives for the disposition of her/his property.

METHODS OF TRANSFERRING PROPERTY AT DEATH

A spouse may use probate or nonprobate transfers or a combination of both to dispose of her/his property at death.

Probate property is property transferred at death by the owner's valid written will. The probate process includes: 1) paying the unpaid obligations or debts of the deceased person; 2) paying the expense incurred in administering the estate such as Personal Representative (or executor) fees, lawyers' fees, and other administrative costs before the remaining property is distributed. Usually, taxes are paid from probate assets.

Property transferred at the death of the owner outside the probate process by operation of law is called nonprobate property. It includes: 1) property held as survivorship marital property; 2) property held in "joint tenancy"; 3) nonprobate property transferred pursuant to the express terms of a marital property agreement; 4) joint and payable on death (POD) accounts in financial institutions; 5) an insurance policy or deferred employment benefit plan with a named beneficiary; 6) U.S. Government bonds with a named co-owner or a payable-on-death (POD) to a named beneficiary; 7) a living trust.

An important characteristic of nonprobate property is that it is not affected by the will of the deceased owner or by the state laws of intestacy.

Generally nonprobate property is not liable for the obligations or debts of the deceased person or for the costs of administering the estate.

Surviving Spouse's Rights in Decedent's Probate Estate

Only the decedent's interest in probate marital property is subject to that person's will. The one-half of the marital property owned by the surviving spouse is *not* a part of the decedent's estate subject to distribution.

The surviving spouse may receive whatever the will provides, if the deceased spouse had a valid will. However, the decedent's will may not provide anything for the surviving spouse. She/he has no entitlement to any portion of the decedent's individual property unless willed to her/him. During the administration of the decedent's estate, marital property, including marital property titled in the name of the surviving spouse and marital property titled in the name of the decedent, is managed by the decedent's Personal Representative. The surviving spouse has certain rights to allowances under most probate codes. Under current law, the Court may award special support allowances to a surviving spouse during administration of the estate and as part of the final distribution of an estate.

Property Transferred by Laws of Intestacy

If a spouse dies without a valid will or the will does not dispose of all of the decedent's probate property, the Wisconsin laws of intestacy dispose of the decedent's probate property or remaining probate property. Under the Marital Property Act the surviving spouse receives all of the decedent's individual property and the decedent's share of marital property if there are no children, or if all children of the decedent are children of the marriage. If the decedent leaves a child or children of a previous marriage, the surviving spouse receives one-half of the decedent's individual property but none of the decedent's share of the marital property. (The one-half of the marital property owned by the surviving spouse is *not* a part of the decedent's estate.) All of the decedent's children share the remaining half of the decedent's individual property and the decedent's share of marital property.

PERSONAL REPRESENTATIVE RESPONSIBILITIES AND RIGHTS

The Personal Representative, the administrator of the decedent's estate, is required to notify a surviving spouse if a beneficiary other than the surviving spouse is designated to receive more than one-half of the proceeds from the decedent's life insurance policy or from a deferred employment benefit plan. The surviving spouse has a right to file a timely claim with the insurance carrier before it makes a distribution of life insurance proceeds. The surviving spouse has the right to recover from the beneficiary one-half of the marital property interest in life insurance proceeds if it is too late to file a claim, and to recover from the beneficiary one-half of the marital property interest in deferred employment benefits.

The Personal Representative must include in the inventory of the decedent's estate the classification of all probate property as marital or individual and the type and amount of any existing obligations. This information is necessary for two reasons: 1) only the decedent's interest in probate marital property is subject to administration; 2) the classification of the obligation determines which property can be reached by creditors to satisfy the obligation.

The Personal Representative may petition the court for a classification of property as either marital or individual. If the Personal Representative and the surviving spouse disagree, the Personal Representative may petition the court for special rights necessary to manage and control marital property during the administration of an estate.

Powers of Guardian of an Incompetent Spouse

If a spouse becomes incompetent and thus unable to exercise her/his legal rights, the Wisconsin guardian chapter authorizes the court to appoint a guardian to manage the property of the incompetent spouse. The Marital Property Act expanded the powers of the guardian to include all management and control rights which the spouse could exercise if the spouse was not subject to guardianship, except the power to make, amend, or revoke a will for the incompetent spouse. The guardian, with court approval, has the authority to participate in transactions when consent or joinder of the incompetent spouse is necessary and to enter into a marital property agreement with the other spouse.

Procedures for Informal Administration of an Estate

The Marital Property Act expanded informal administration procedures. One summary confirmation procedure simplifies establishment of ownership of survivorship marital property and of property transferred by a marital property agreement. The Personal Representative of the decedent may file with the Probate Registrar a verified statement describing the property transferred by survivorship marital property and/or the property transferred by a marital property agreement. The verified statement has the same effect as a certificate issued by the court.

The other summary confirmation procedure simplifies documentation of specified nonprobate property transfers. The person having the right to survivorship marital property or the right to property transferred by a marital property agreement may petition the court. The certificate issued by the court establishes the petitioner's interest in the property.

The summary confirmation procedures apply not only to a designated person, trust, or other entity having an interest in any property passing by nontestamentary disposition under a marital property agreement, but also to any other interest of the surviving spouse in the decedent's property.

Economic Protections of the Surviving Spouse

The Marital Property Act provides economic protections for the surviving spouse that were not available under prior Wisconsin law based on the separate property system. Unless there have been modifications by the spouses, these economic protections include: 1) one-half of each and every item of marital property is owned automatically by the surviving spouse by operation of law; 2) the surviving spouse has a marital property interest in the proceeds of any life insurance policy owned by the decedent that has a marital property component; 3) a surviving spouse has a marital property interest in the marital property component of the decedent's pension or deferred employment benefit plan; 4) a surviving spouse may recover in a court action gifts of marital property given without her/his consent which exeed the gift limit set by law; 5) the surviving spouse has the right to receive the entire net probate estate if the decedent spouse died without a valid will and all of the decedent's children are also children of the surviving spouse; 6) the surviving spouse has a right to receive one-half of the decedent's individual property if the decedent leaves a child or children from a prior marriage and the decedent died without a will; and 7) in addition, special protection of a surviving spouse in hardship circumstances is provided.

The Marital Property Act gives the court the authority to provide a special allowance to support a needy surviving spouse as long as necessary. The court may set aside the portion of the decedent's estate needed for such support before giving the property to creditors, heirs, and beneficiaries. The right of the court to provide permanent support for the surviving spouse in hardship cases exists whether the decedent died with or without a will.

Marital Property Tax Advantage

Appreciated marital property and appreciated survivorship marital property receive a favorable capital gains tax treatment under both federal and state income tax laws. At the death of a spouse both halves of the marital property owned by the decedent and the surviving spouse, receive a "stepped-up" basis equal to the market value of the property on the decedent's date of death.

If sometime after the death of a spouse appreciated marital property is sold, the capital gains tax is calculated on the difference between the value of the property on the disposition or sale date and the value of the entire property on the decedent's date of death—its "stepped-up" basis.

A different method is used to calculate the capital gains tax on the sale of appreciated property held exclusively by husband and wife as "joint tenants" or as "tenants-in-common." Only the decedent's one-half interest in "joint tenancy" or "tenancy-in-common" property receives a "stepped-up" basis to the market value of the property on the decedent's date of death. The one-half interest owned by the surviving spouse retains its original basis (acquisition cost). If sometime after the decedent's death the appreciated property held as "joint tenants" or "tenants-in-common" is disposed of, the capital gains tax is calculated on the difference between the value of the property on the disposition date and the original basis for the one-half owned by the surviving spouse and the "stepped-up" or date-of-death basis for the one-half owned by the decedent's estate.

Estate Planning for Disposition of Property at Death of a Spouse

Typically, both husband and wife own marital property and individual property under Wisconsin's marital property system. Hence, each spouse needs to think through how to dispose of this property at death.

Estate planning should begin with an inventory of property owned by a spouse, its classification as marital or individual property, and its characterization as probate or nonprobate property. This provides a spouse with a comprehensive picture of the composition of her/his estate.

Each spouse may wish to explore creative estate planning and the use of nonprobate methods of transferring property such as holding property by document of title as survivorship marital property, or transferring nonprobate property by a marital property agreement.

A valid will is essential if a spouse wants to: 1) decide who will receive her/his probate property at death; 2) nominate a Personal Representative to administer her/his estate; 3) nominate a guardian for her/his minor children.

With this background information, a spouse can define and clarify personal goals for the disposition of property at death and select the appropriate legal mechanisms for achieving those goals.

Marital Property Agreements

Overview

Marital property agreements add important flexibility to the marital property system in Wisconsin. There are two kinds of marital property agreements, "regular" and "special" (also called statutory). The "regular" agreement enables a married couple to design an agreement that best suits their particular situation. Two "special" or statutory marital property agreement forms were designed and added by the 1988 amendments of the Marital Property Act. To be valid and enforceable in a court of law, both "regular" and "special" agreements must comply with the requirements specified by law.

Definition and Purpose

If the statutory rules of sharing income and property acquired during marriage through the efforts of both spouses do not fit the needs and circumstances of a married couple, the spouses have contractual freedom to vary most provisions of the Marital Property Act. They have the legal right to develop their own contracts governing the economic aspects of their ongoing marriage and the disposition of property at death.

The "regular" marital property agreement is a legal contract between husband and wife enforceable in a court of law that deals only with property rights and/or obligations of the spouses. It is a written document signed by husband and wife and only those parties.

A married couple may use as many agreements as necessary to achieve their goals. A marital property agreement may be general or comprehensive in scope and cover a broad range of subjects, or specific and even limited to one asset.

"Regular" Marital Property Agreement Subjects

The subjects that a "regular" marital property agreement may cover are listed in broad categories in the Marital Property Act. Most of the economic aspects of an ongoing marriage, including ownership, management and control of marital property and even the support of a spouse, may be varied. Disposition of marital and individual property without probate at the death of a spouse may be provided for in a marital property agreement.

Support of a spouse during marriage may be modified or eliminated by a marital property agreement. Such modification or elimination, however, may not result in a spouse having less than necessary and adequate support, taking into consideration all sources of support. Also, the marital property agreement may not create eligibility for public assistance at the death of a spouse or at the time of divorce. A marital property agreement covering post-divorce support is considered by, although it is not binding, on a court at divorce.

If a marital property agreement classifies as marital property the noninsured spouse's interest in a life insurance policy which designates the other spouse as the owner and insured, and the noninsured spouse dies before the insured spouse, the "frozen interest" rule applies to the marital property interest of the noninsured spouse, unless the marital property agreement expressly provides otherwise. This rule clarifies the value of the decedent's marital property interest in the policy on the decedent's date of death.

A marital property agreement may be used to create a "joint tenancy" or a "tenancy-in-common" form of property ownership exclusively between husband and wife if the spouses prefer these forms of ownership to survivorship marital property or marital property.

Restrictions on "Regular" Marital Property Agreement Subjects

A "regular" marital property agreement may not vary these provisions of the Marital Property Act: 1) the right of a child to support including a court-ordered child support obligation of either spouse; 2) the duty of each spouse to act in "good faith" in the management and control of marital property and each other's individual property; 3) the protection of "bona fide purchasers" of marital property; 4) the rights of creditors.

Legal Requirements of Valid "Regular" Marital Property Agreements

The legal requirements of a valid "regular" marital property agreement are: 1) the agreement must be in writing (oral agreements are not enforceable); 2) the agreement must be signed by both husband and wife; 3) there must be fair and reasonable disclosure of each spouse's assets and liabilities "under the circumstances" (this flexible standard is designed to take into account the extent to which property rights are being changed knowingly by the agreement); 4) the agreement cannot be unconscionable when made (grossly unfair or extremely one-sided); and 5) the agreement must be entered into voluntarily (free from coercion or undue influence).

The statutory financial disclosure form provided for the newly created "special" type of statutory property classification agreements is *not* required for a "regular" marital property agreement.

There is no legal requirement that the signatures of the spouses be witnessed or notarized or that it be recorded in the office of the county Registrar of Deeds. A married couple may want to record a marital property agreement to establish proof of its existence. Recording a marital property agreement does not affect other persons unless the agreement affects real estate in the county of record, has a legal description of the real estate, and complies with all recording requirements for documents affecting real estate interests.

Who May Make a "Regular" Marital Property Agreement and When

A "regular" marital property agreement may be made by: 1) a married couple (they may negotiate and sign one or more marital property agreements any time during marriage); 2) persons intending to marry (they may negotiate and sign a marital property agreement before marriage, but the agreement becomes effective only when they marry); and 3) a court-appointed guardian of an incompetent spouse whom the law authorizes to sign a marital property agreement for that spouse subject to court approval.

Drafting a "Regular" Marital Property Agreement

The law does not require a couple to hire a lawyer to draft a "regular" marital property agreement. If both spouses are knowledgeable about financial matters, well informed about their rights and obligations under the Marital Property Act, and familiar with writing legally binding documents, they may draft and sign their marital property agreement without a lawyer. To make certain that their marital property agreement is valid and meets their needs, one or both spouses may choose to have a lawyer review their agreement.

If one spouse is not as knowledgeable as the other about legal and financial matters, the couple may wish to consult an attorney about the legal, economic, and tax consequences of the marital property agreement before the agreement is drafted.

One or both spouses may choose to have a lawyer draft a "regular" marital property agreement. There is no requirement that each spouse have independent counsel (different lawyers), but use of separate attorneys increases the likelihood that a court will enforce the agreement. If there are provisions in the marital property agreement relating to divorce, separate attorneys are essential.

In situations where one spouse is giving up valuable property rights or is assuming heavy obligations, or where one spouse is very inexperienced in financial or legal matters, or where there is family discord, separate legal representation of each spouse is desirable and may be necessary to ensure enforceability of a "regular" marital property agreement.

CHANGING A "REGULAR" MARITAL PROPERTY AGREEMENT

If a couple's marriage is on-going or intact, the *only* way to change (amend or revoke) a "regular" marital property agreement is to make a new agreement. Neither spouse has the right to amend or revoke a "regular" agreement unilaterally (without consent of the other spouse). Both husband and wife must act together to amend or revoke a "regular" agreement by writing and signing a new agreement. Tearing up or burning a marital property agreement does not revoke it.

However, if a marriage is ended by divorce, the divorce revokes a marital property agreement. A provision in a marital property agreement that provides upon the death of either spouse any of either or both spouse's property passes without probate to a designated person, trust, or other entity by nontestamentary disposition is revoked upon dissolution of the marriage, as a matter of law, upon a judgment of annulment, divorce, or legal separation, unless the judgment provides otherwise.

"REGULAR" MARITAL PROPERTY AGREEMENTS AS FINANCIAL PLANNING TOOLS

The statutory right of husband and wife to contract with each other in a "regular" marital property agreement provides a new financial planning tool. Some examples of what a marital property agreement can do are to: 1) make certain that some or all of the property from a spouse's previous marriage goes to the children of that marriage; 2) reclassify marital property as individual property; 3) avoid probate by providing that some or all property belonging to either spouse pass without probate at the death of the first spouse or at the death of the second spouse or both; 4) reduce the capital gains tax liability on appreciated individual property sold after the death of a spouse by reclassifying individual property as marital property or survivorship marital property; 5) limit the state income tax liability of a spouse by filing a copy of the marital property agreement with the Wisconsin Department of Revenue before any tax assessment is made. The Department of Revenue is bound by the provisions of a marital property agreement as long as both spouses are domiciled in Wisconsin.

Characteristics of "Special" or Statutory Marital Property Agreement Forms

The "special" or statutory marital property agreements created by the 1988 amendments to the Marital Property Act are rigidly defined agreements. The two statutory marital property agreement forms provided are: 1) a statutory terminable marital property classification agreement form; 2) a statutory terminable individual property classification agreement form. In these statutory forms: 1) the text or wording of the property classification agreement is defined; 2) the financial disclosure form is prescribed; 3) the text or wording of the termination form is defined. If the statutory agreement form is altered or changed in any way, the agreement is not legally effective.

Statutory Terminable Marital Property Classification Agreement: Definition and Purpose

The statutory terminable marital property classification agreement is a comprehensive statutory agreement form executed by husband and wife to classify all the property presently owned by them and all the property acquired or created in the future as marital property. The statutory agreement form determines the ownership of all property of the spouses during marriage and at the death of a spouse. A couple about to marry may execute this statutory form which becomes effective upon their marriage.

Spouses who believe in the legal principle of automatic sharing of property acquired during marriage may find this comprehensive agreement form a simple and convenient method of reclassifying their individual and "unclassified" property as marital property. (Chapter 6 explains "unclassified" property.) Joint accounts and marital accounts in financial institutions are not affected by a statutory terminable marital property classification agreement form.

Statutory Terminable Individual Property Classification Agreement: Definition and Purpose

The statutory terminable individual property classification agreement is a statutory agreement form executed by husband and wife to classify the marital property presently owned by them, and property acquired or created in the future that would otherwise be marital property, as the individual property of the owner spouse. Only marital property acquired after the marital property system became effective for them is reclassified by this agreement form. Any "unclassified" property which the couple may own is *not* reclassified by this agreement form. A couple about to marry may execute this statutory form which becomes effective upon their marriage.

If the rules of automatic sharing of marital property do not fit the needs and circumstances of a married couple, the statutory agreement form to reclassify their marital property as individual property may provide a simple statutory alternative to the mandatory marital property system.

During the lifetime of the spouses the owner spouse has the exclusive right to manage and control individual property. At the death of the owner spouse some special rights are given to the surviving spouse as to property of the decedent spouse which has been reclassified by the agreement. The surviving spouse has certain "elective" rights in the decedent's probate "deferred" marital property and in the decedent's nonprobate augmented marital property estate. Property acquired while the statutory agreement is in effect, which would have been marital property but for the agreement, is classified as "deferred" marital property. (Chapter 6 explains "deferred" marital property and the augmented marital property estate.) A joint bank account, including the incident of survivorship, held in a financial institution is not affected by a statutory terminable individual property classification agreement form.

Legal Requirements of a Valid Statutory Property Classification Agreement

There are four requirements for a valid statutory property classification agreement: 1) the statutory agreement form must contain language identical to the form set forth in the statute; 2) the financial disclosure form prescribed in the statute must be completed and attached to the statutory agreement form to avoid limiting the duration of the agreement; 3) the agreement must be signed by both spouses; 4) the signature of each spouse must be authenticated by a Wisconsin lawyer or acknowledged before a Wisconsin notary public.

If the statutory property classification agreement form is altered or changed in any way, the agreement is not legally effective.

Financial Disclosure and Duration of Statutory Property Classification Agreement

A statutory property classification agreement is effective for a maximum period of three years unless there has been adequate disclosure of each spouse's assets and financial obligations.

If the spouses do not complete satisfactorily the financial disclosure form prescribed in the statute before executing the agreement or contemporaneously with the execution of the agreement, the agreement terminates automatically three years after the date both spouses signed the agreement, unless one spouse terminated the agreement earlier.

The rules also state that a statutory property classification agreement without complete disclosure of the spouses' assets and financial obligations may be used only once. If the financial disclosure form prescribed by statute is completed satisfactorily and attached to the statutory property classification agreement form, the agreement terminates at the death of the first spouse unless terminated earlier by one of the spouses.

Even though a completed financial disclosure form is attached to the statutory agreement, if later legal action is taken by one spouse to enforce the statutory property classification agreement and it is established that the information on the financial disclosure form did not provide fair and reasonable disclosure "under the circumstance" of the assets or financial obligations of the other spouse, the maximum duration of the agreement is three years after both spouses signed the agreement. This limitation on the duration of the agreement applies only when it is established that fair and reasonable disclosure of assets and obligations was not made by a spouse.

TERMINATION OF STATUTORY PROPERTY CLASSIFICATION AGREEMENTS

One spouse may unilaterally (without consent of the other spouse) terminate a statutory property classification agreement at any time by executing the termination form set forth in the statute. The agreement terminates 30 days after notice of termination is given to the other spouse. Notice of termination is given the other spouse on the date that: 1) a signed termination form is personally delivered to the other spouse; 2) a signed termination form is sent by the spouse giving notice by certified mail to the last known address of the other spouse.

If a statutory individual property classification agreement is terminated, a special provision of the law applies to both spouses.

After notice of termination is given and until the termination date becomes effective, each spouse shall act in "good faith" with respect to the other in matters involving the property of the acting spouse classified as individual property by the agreement.

Termination of a statutory property classification agreement is prospective. It applies only to the future. The classification of property acquired before the termination date becomes effective is not affected by the termination of the agreement. Property acquired after the effective termination date is classified by statutory definition as marital property or individual property, or according to the provisions of a new or other "regular" marital property agreement.

Termination of a statutory property classification agreement as it affects third parties is treated in the same manner as termination of a marital property agreement.

Termination of a statutory property classification agreement does not affect the ability of spouses to amend, revoke, or supplement a statutory agreement by a "regular" marital property agreement.

"Notices" in the Statutory Property Classification Agreement Form

A specific "Notice" appropriate for each type of statutory agreement is part of and precedes the statutory agreement form. The purpose of the "Notice" is to make persons interested in either of these forms aware of property rights that will be affected by the agreement. Each person should read the "Notice" carefully and if there are questions, seek legal counsel before signing a statutory property classification agreement form.

The lengthy "Notice" covers these subjects:

1. Brief explanation of Wisconsin Marital Property Law
2. Rights relinquished and rights acquired
3. Effect on: a) credit and obligations; b) management and control of property; c) disposition of property by will; d) taxes; e) previous marriage agreement
4. Effect on a) legal duty of support; b) divorce

5. Effect on automatic and elective rights of surviving spouse (Individual Property Classification Agreement only)
6. Effect on creditors
7. Effect on real estate
8. Financial disclosure and duration of agreement
9. Termination rights
10. Effect of termination on classification of property
11. Right to amend, revoke, or supplement a statutory agreement
12. Signature of both spouses required and each signature must be authenticated
13. Need to retain a copy of the statutory agreement form, the financial disclosure form, and the termination form, if used
14. Need for legal counsel if one or both spouses is domiciled outside of Wisconsin

Spousal Rights Not Affected by Statutory Property Classification Agreements

A statutory property classification agreement does not affect the spouses' duty to support each other. Neither does it affect property division and maintenance payments at divorce.

Statutory Property Classification Agreement Effect on Creditors

In general, statutory property classification agreements are not binding on creditors unless the creditor is furnished a copy of the agreement before credit is extended. It is not necessary to furnish a copy of the financial disclosure form.

CHAPTER 6 ⚜

Property Rights of Spouses During Transition from the Separate to the Marital Property System

Overview

The 1984 Marital Property Act provided for an orderly transition from Wisconsin's separate property system to its newly adopted marital property system. The legal concepts that bridge the two systems are: 1) "unclassified" property; 2) "deferred" marital property; and 3) "elective" rights of the surviving spouse in "deferred" marital property. These mechanisms were necessary because if the state legislature passed a state law that changed the property ownership rights of spouses and made the changes retroactive, the law might be declared unconstitutional. To eliminate this risk while providing protections for surviving spouses in property acquired by the decedent spouse during marriage but prior to the Act's effective date, the 1984 Marital Property Act provides legal mechanisms to bridge the two property systems.

Only couples who were married and living in Wisconsin before 1986 and married couples who lived in another state and moved to Wisconsin after 1985 are affected by the provisions of the Marital Property Act covered in Chapter 6.

Couples who were married and domiciled in Wisconsin before January 1, 1986, and who continue to be domiciled in Wisconsin need to be informed about the Marital Property Act provisions covered in Chapter 5 and Chapter 6. Married couples who lived in another state and move to Wisconsin after 1985, will need to be informed about the Marital Property Act provisions covered in Chapter 5, Chapter 6, and Chapter 7.

"Unclassified" Property

Only Wisconsin couples who were married and domiciled in Wisconsin before 1986, and married couples who lived in another state and moved to Wisconsin after 1985, and both spouses establish a Wisconsin domicile, own "unclassified" property under the Marital Property Act. Couples who marry on or after January 1, 1986, and remain domiciled in Wisconsin thereafter do *not* own any "unclassified" property. All the property they bring to their marriage (their determination date) is individual property.

Married couples who own "unclassified" property need to know that pre-determination date property acquired during marriage by gift or inheritance and property brought to the marriage are "unclassified" property, which is treated like individual property during their marriage. When the owning spouse dies first, this property which "would have been individual property" is not subject to the surviving spouse's "deferred" marital property elections. Although "would have been individual property" has no special statutory name, it is commonly referred to as "deferred" individual property. Only the property which spouses receive by gift or inheritance after their determination date is classified as individual property by the Marital Property Act.

Statutory Definition

"Unclassified" property is property which a couple married and domiciled in Wisconsin before January 1, 1986, owned on that date. On January 1, 1986, when the marital property system became effective, "unclassified" property remained "unclassified." When the first spouse dies, it may become necessary to classify the decedent's "unclassified" property into: 1) "deferred" marital property; or 2) "deferred" individual property.

By statutory definition, "deferred" marital property is that portion of the decedent spouse's "unclassified" property that would have been marital property if the Marital Property Act had been in effect when the property was acquired. The rules governing the rights of the surviving spouse in "deferred" marital property become effective only when the owner spouse dies first.

"Deferred" individual property is that portion of "unclassified" property which is not "deferred" marital property. The estate of the owner spouse must be able to trace and document any "deferred" individual property. At the death of the owner spouse, "deferred" individual property is not subject to the "elective" rights of the surviving spouse.

OWNERSHIP DETERMINATION

Document of title to the property determines ownership of "unclassified" property. The spouse whose name is on the document of title is the owner of that "unclassified" property. The property system in effect in Wisconsin through December 31, 1985, was called the title-based property system, as well as the separate property system. Ownership of untitled property is determined by which spouse supplied the funds to purchase the item, except for property inherited or gifted to a spouse.

STATUTORY PRESUMPTION

The Marital Property Act presumes that all "unclassified" property of the first spouse to die is "deferred" marital property. This statutory presumption may be rebutted by evidence to prove that the funds used to acquire the "unclassified" property were "deferred" individual property. The person who wishes to establish "deferred" individual property ownership rights in "unclassified" property is responsible for providing the documentation necessary to trace the property back to its original source of funds. If the "deferred" individual property classification cannot be established for part or all of the "unclassified" property, the entire "unclassified" property asset will be classified as "deferred" marital property.

RIGHTS OF OWNER SPOUSE

The owner of "unclassified" property has the exclusive right to manage and control that property during her/his lifetime. "Unclassified" property is treated "as if" it were the individual property of the titled spouse.

The titled spouse has the right to dispose of her/his "unclassified" probate property by will except for the "elective" rights of the surviving spouse in the decedent's "unclassified" probate property. "Unclassified" probate property subject to the decedent's will includes: 1) all "deferred" individual probate property; 2) all "deferred" marital probate property that is *not* subject to the "elective" rights of the surviving spouse.

The titled spouse who owns a business with both an "unclassified" component and a marital property component has the right to sign a directive that requires satisfaction of the surviving spouse's marital property or "elective" "deferred" marital property interest with other property of the deceased titled spouse of equal value.

The management and control option of the holding or managing spouse to direct the settlement of the marital property interest of the nonholding spouse was created by a 1988 amendment to the Marital Property Act. The option applies only to certain types of business: 1) an interest in a partnership held as a general partner or an interest in a joint venture held as a participant; 2) an interest in a professional corporation, professional association, or similar entity held as a stockholder or member; and 3) an interest in a corporation the stock of which is not publicly traded.

MIXED PROPERTY

"Unclassified" property (either "deferred" marital property or "deferred" individual property) with a marital property component is mixed property. A marital property component may be created by post-determination date income or "fruits" of "unclassified" property. The "deferred" marital property component may occur in: 1) a business owned solely by the decedent spouse before 1986; 2) the decedent spouse's "straddle" life insurance policy (explained later); 3) the decedent spouse's "straddle" deferred employment benefit plan (explained later).

INCOME RECLASSIFICATION

By statutory definition, marital property is income or "fruits" (dividends, interest, net rents) of "unclassified" property earned or paid on or after January 1, 1986. If the dividends of corporate stock acquired before 1986 ("unclassified" property) are reinvested to purchase additional shares of stock, mixed property may be created.

The owner spouse has the legal right to unilaterally (without permission or agreement of the nonowning spouse) reclassify post-determination date income or "fruits" of "unclassified" property from marital property to individual property. To achieve this reclassification, the owner spouse must: 1) declare in writing that the income or "fruits" of "unclassified" property is individual property and sign the statement; 2) have the statement acknowledged by a notary; 3) give notice of the statement to the nonowning spouse. Within five days of execution the notice must be delivered to the nonowning spouse or be sent by certified mail to the nonowning spouse's last known address. By this action the owner spouse of "unclassified" property can avoid creating mixed property.

The unilateral statement is prospective only. It applies to the future. Only the income or "fruits" of "unclassified" property earned or paid after the effective date of the unilateral statement will be reclassified as individual property. A unilateral statement may not be used to reclassify income or "fruits" of "unclassified" property that accrued prior to January 1, 1986, or that accrued prior to the effective date of the unilateral statement. A marital property agreement may be used to reclassify income or "fruits" of "unclassified" property that accrued before 1986 or before the effective date of the unilateral statement.

BUSINESS PROPERTY

A business owned solely by one spouse before 1986 that continues in operation after 1985 is "unclassified" property. It remains "unclassified" property during the lifetime of the owner spouse unless the owner spouse chooses to reclassify it. The owner spouse has the exclusive right to manage and control the business.

However, a marital property component or a "deferred" marital property component, or both, may be created if either or both spouses worked in the business either before 1986 or after 1985 or during both periods.

If either the owner spouse or the nonowning spouse, or both, work in the business ("unclassified" property), the income they earn after 1985 by either or both is marital property under the Marital Property Act. If post-1985 earned income (profits) are reinvested in the business, the business becomes mixed property. That part of the business attributable to the reinvestment of income earned after 1985 will be marital property. The spouse who previously had no ownership interest in the business will now have a marital property interest in the marital property component of the business.

If a substantial increase in the value of the business after 1985 is due to the substantial effort of either or both spouses, the "active" appreciation may be marital property. The amount of appreciation due to the substantial effort of a spouse is marital property unless reasonable compensation was received by the spouse whose effort resulted in the property appreciation. If reasonable compensation was received, there is no marital property component, and the appreciation after 1985 is "unclassified" property. If reasonable compensation was not received, the spouse who previously had no ownership interest in the business will now have a marital property interest in the marital property component.

If a substantial increase in the value of the "unclassified" property business after 1985 is due to inflationary or market forces without any effort of the owner or the nonowning spouse, that increase is considered "passive" appreciation and remains "unclassified" property.

An "unclassified" property business owned solely by one spouse before 1986 that continues in operation after 1985 may have a "deferred" marital property component. If a spouse worked in the business before 1986, her/his earned income would be classified as "deferred" marital property if that spouse died first. If that earned income (profits) was reinvested in the business, that portion of the business attributable to the reinvestment of the profits would be "deferred" marital property if the spouse owning the business died first.

If there was a substantial increase in the value of the business before 1986 due to the substantial effort of the owning spouse without reasonable compensation, the "active" appreciation in the value of the business would be "deferred" marital property, if the owning spouse died first.

If the funds used to acquire the business before 1986 would have been marital property if the business had been acquired after 1985, that portion of the business attributable to the acquisition funds would be "deferred" marital property if the owning spouse died first.

If the decedent spouse left a will, her/his "unclassified" business property must be classified at her/his death. Classification will determine whether a "deferred" marital property component or a "deferred" individual property component, or both, exist.

STRADDLE LIFE INSURANCE POLICY

If a life insurance policy was issued before January 1, 1986 with the insured person designated as owner, and the policy continues in effect after that date and the insured spouse is the first spouse to die, it is a "straddle" policy. As soon as one premium is paid with marital property, either by the spouse or the spouse's employer, the policy becomes mixed property. The new marital property classification continues even if all later premiums are paid with nonmarital property.

A life insurance policy classified as "mixed" property may have both a marital property and a nonmarital property component, including "unclassified" property. At the death of the insured spouse, a statutory formula determines what portion of the proceeds is marital property and what portion is nonmarital property. The surviving spouse has a right to one-half of the proceeds classified as marital property, regardless of the named beneficiary, and may have certain "elective" rights in the unclassified property component which is classified as "deferred" marital property.

The noninsured spouse may release her/his marital property interest in the premiums or proceeds, or both, and "deferred" marital property "elective" rights in the proceeds of a "straddle" life insurance policy by: 1) a written consent statement; 2) a marital property agreement. A written consent statement must be carefully drafted if the noninsured spouse wishes to avoid adverse gift tax consequences. Even if the named beneficiary is the parent or child of either spouse, written consent by the noninsured spouse is required in order for the named beneficiary to receive all of the proceeds. A written consent statement may be revoked unless it contains a statement specifying it is irrevocable.

Straddle Deferred Employment Benefit Plan

If a deferred employment benefit plan is the result of the employment of a spouse partly before and partly after January 1, 1986, it is a "straddle plan." It straddles both the separate property system and the marital property system. It is classified as mixed property with both a marital property component and a nonmarital property, including the "unclassified" property component, if the employment began before the couple's determination date. A statutory formula prorates the plan's classification of property based upon the length of employment. The marital property interest of the nonemployee spouse is one-half of the marital property component of a deferred employment benefit plan. If the nonemployee spouse dies before the employee spouse, the "frozen interest" rule applies to the marital property interest of the nonemployee spouse, unless a marital property agreement provides otherwise. This rule clarifies the value of the decedent's marital property interest in a plan on the decedent's date of death.

If the nonemployee spouse dies first, the nonemployee spouse's marital property interest terminates.

Federal rules govern the property rights of spouses in many private deferred employment benefit plans, and may preempt the Wisconsin Marital Property Act rules. The Federal Employee Retirement Income Security Act (ERISA) was amended by the Federal Retirement Equity Act of 1984 (REA). The REA amendments deal with pre-retirement and post-retirement benefits. One amendment provides that 50 percent of the pre-retirement death benefits covered by law must be paid to the surviving spouse regardless of the designated beneficiary at the time of death, unless the surviving spouse has consented in writing to another designated beneficiary.

The other amendment covers post-retirement benefits. If both spouses are living at the time the employee spouse retires, there are rules governing the pension plan. A pension plan that provides retirement benefits to a married person must provide for a husband and wife pension or joint and survivor benefits. The income from the pension must cover the lives of the employee and the employee's spouse, unless written consent to choose another plan has been given by the spouse of the employee. The federal legislation specifies the required consent form.

PROPERTY HELD JOINTLY BY HUSBAND AND WIFE

Property held in "joint tenancy" by document of title exclusively by husband and wife before January 1, 1986, is "unclassified" property. The right of survivorship that is part of "joint tenancy" ownership is not affected by the Marital Property Act, even if marital property is added to or mixed into this "joint tenancy" after December 31, 1985.

During the lifetime of the parties to a "joint tenancy," one joint tenant has the legal right unilaterally (without consent of the other tenant) to sever the "joint tenancy" and thus eliminate the right of survivorship, except for a homestead held in "joint tenancy." The severance action may be taken by one spouse without notification to the other spouse and creates a "tenancy-in-common" form of property ownership.

The Marital Property Act did not affect the right of survivorship to a homestead held as "joint tenants" exclusively between husband and wife by document of title before January 1, 1986. The entire property is automatically owned by the surviving spouse by operation of law without probate. The Act also did not affect the Wisconsin homestead joinder rule which states that spouses must join in the sale, gifting, or mortgaging of their homestead regardless of which one owns the property.

Property held as "tenants-in-common" by document of title exclusively between husband and wife before January 1, 1986, is "unclassified" property. The Marital Property Act did not change the ownership rights of the spouses. Each spouse has an equal undivided interest in property held as "tenants-in-common" and the right to will one-half of it. In the absence of a valid will, the decedent's interest in such a "tenancy-in-common" passes under the laws of intestacy.

Property Held Jointly by a Married Person and a Third Party

Property held in "joint tenancy" by document of title by a married person and a third party before January 1, 1986, continues to be "joint tenancy" property. The right of survivorship of any "joint tenancy" created before January 1, 1986, was not changed by the Marital Property Act.

At the death of the married person, the surviving spouse may have certain "elective" rights if the property held in "joint tenancy" by the decedent spouse with a third party before January 1, 1986, would have been "deferred" marital property in whole or in part.

Property held as "tenants-in-common" by document of title by a married person and a third party before January 1, 1986, continues as a "tenancy-in-common." The ownership rights of "tenants-in-common" were not changed by the Marital Property Act. The married person has an undivided interest in the property held as "tenants-in-common" and the right to will that interest at death.

At the death of the married person, the surviving spouse may have certain "elective" rights if the property held as "tenants-in-common" with a third party before January 1, 1986, would have been "deferred" marital property.

In the absence of a valid will the decedent's interest in the property held as "tenants-in-common" passes under the laws of intestacy.

"Elective" Rights of Surviving Spouse

"Elective" rights of the surviving spouse in "deferred" marital property make certain that the surviving spouse receives an equitable share of the "unclassified" property owned by the decedent spouse. The "elective" rights of the surviving spouse in "deferred" marital property provided by the 1984 Marital Property Act replace the "elective" share of one-third of the decedent's net probate estate to which the surviving spouse was entitled under the separate property system in effect in Wisconsin through December 31, 1985. The Marital Property Act provides the surviving spouse with "elective" rights to receive up to one-half of the decedent's probate and nonprobate "deferred" marital property. However, if a surviving spouse does not elect "deferred" probate marital property, there is no transfer of property, and no gift is made by the surviving spouse.

If the deceased spouse leaves a valid will, the surviving spouse usually may receive whatever the will provides and may have "elective" rights to one-half of the "deferred" marital property in the decedent's probate estate. A surviving spouse's right to elect "deferred" marital property is intended to apply even to the decedent's real property located in another state. The decedent's will may require, however, that the surviving spouse choose between the share provided for her/him in the will and her/his "elective" rights in the decedent's probate "deferred" marital property.

The augmented marital property estate protects the surviving spouse from nonprobate transfers of "deferred" marital property to third parties that defeat the surviving spouse's "elective" rights in probate "deferred" marital property. If the decedent spouse made nonprobate transfers of "deferred" marital property to third parties on or after April 4, 1984 (the date the Governor signed the Marital Property Act) without the consent of the surviving spouse, the surviving spouse has the right to elect up to 50 percent of the value of specified types of nonprobate "deferred" marital property. If the surviving spouse does not seek reimbursement from a person who is liable for contribution as a result of an election in the augmented marital property estate by the surviving spouse, there is no transfer of property, and no gift made by the surviving spouse to the person liable for contribution.

If the surviving spouse received a "fair share" (at least one-half of the decedent's combined probate and nonprobate property), the "elective" right in probate "deferred" marital property is eliminated. If the surviving spouse received property from the decedent during her/his lifetime or at death, the "elective" right to one-half of the "deferred" marital property in the decedent's augmented marital property estate is reduced by such transfers.

The court may direct that the special support allowances to a surviving spouse during the administration of the estate and as part of the final distribution of an estate be applied to the "elective" rights of the surviving spouse in "deferred" marital property and in the augmented marital property estate. If the court does not so direct, the allowance is not charged against the "elective" rights of the surviving spouse.

The "elective" rights of the surviving spouse are not automatic. Whether or not to exercise those "elective" rights is a decision the surviving spouse must make and implement in a timely way. To implement "elective" rights the surviving spouse must file a written document with the court within six months of the decedent's death asserting her/his "elective" rights to the decedent's probate "deferred" marital property, and/or the decedent's augmented marital property estate. In addition, the surviving spouse is required to commence a separate court action within three months of filing an election against the decedent's augmented marital property estate.

"Deferred" marital property elected by the surviving spouse, except to the extent that no other property is available to satisfy the obligation, is not subject to claims for the decedent's funeral expense, federal death taxes against the decedent's estate, or state taxes against the decedent's estate.

Property Disposition by Laws of Intestacy

If the titled spouse of "unclassified" property dies without a will (intestate), the Marital Property Act provides that the surviving spouse receives all of the decedent's net probate estate including all "unclassified" property, if the decedent has no children, or if all of the children are children of this marriage.

If there is one or more children from a previous marriage, the surviving spouse's share of one-half of the decedent's "unclassified" "deferred" marital property is now automatic rather than elective. (The surviving spouse also receives one-half of the decedent's other nonmarital property, including individual property and "deferred" individual property.) The 1992 change, which eliminated any need for the surviving spouse to elect in order to receive "deferred" marital property under intestacy, simplifies probate administration, and is consistent with the intestacy rule when there are no issue of the decedent or when the surviving issue are all issue of the surviving spouse and the decedent. All children of the decedent share the other half of the decedent's interest in "unclassified" marital property, the other half of the decedent's individual property, and the decedent's one-half interest in marital property.

Review of Will and Estate Plans

The Marital Property Act may have unanticipated or unintended effects on a spouse's will and estate plan if the will and the estate plan were based on Wisconsin's prior separate property system. Each spouse needs to review her/his will and estate plan to determine the effects, if any, of the Marital Property Act.

The "elective" rights of a surviving spouse in "deferred" probate and nonprobate marital property may affect the distribution of "unclassified" property if the owner spouse dies first. Equal ownership rights of each spouse in marital property acquired after January 1, 1986, and the new forms of holding property jointly between husband and wife by document of title as marital property or survivorship marital property may result in a spouse having more or less property than previously to dispose of by will. Spouses owning "unclassified" property may wish to simplify their estate planning and administration by reclassifying such property to reduce or eliminate classification issues. These couples may wish to explore the use of nonprobate methods of transferring property, such as a marital property agreement.

Married couples who own both "unclassified" property and marital property need a complete picture of all of their property in order to review and revise their wills, if needed. This would include the amount of "unclassified" property ("deferred" marital property and "deferred" individual property), and the amount of marital property and individual property owned by each spouse. The additional division of property into probate and nonprobate property completes the basic information needed for creative and desired estate planning.

CHAPTER 7 ✣

Property Rights of Mobile Married Couples Who Move from Another State to Wisconsin After 1985

The provisions of the Marital Property Act apply to mobile married couples who move from another state to Wisconsin after 1985 on their determination date, the date on which *both* spouses become domiciled in Wisconsin. If only one spouse is domiciled in Wisconsin, the Marital Property Act does not generally govern the property rights of either spouse.

Property acquired by mobile married couples while domiciled in another state and in Wisconsin before their determination date, is "unclassified" property. The rights of the owner spouse of "unclassified" property, including the right to reclassify or gift it, and the "elective" rights of the surviving spouse if the owner spouse dies first, are explained in Chapter 6 and not repeated in Chapter 7. Mobile married couples need to become informed about the provisions of the Marital Property Act explained in Chapter 5, as well as those in Chapter 6. A review of their wills and estate plans is highly desirable. A spouse who does not have a will should become familiar with Wisconsin's laws of intestacy to know how her/his probate property will be distributed at her/his death.

Part III ✣

CHAPTER 8 ✦

The 1998 Amendments to the Probate Code

Overview

The 1998 Amendments to the Probate Code are the first major revisions of the Probate Code since 1969. The extensive revisions simplify, clarify, refine and re-define provisions of the Probate Code. A new section that contains general rules applicable to both probate and nonprobate property transfers was created. Many of the revisions in Chapter 861 of the Probate Code relate to protections of the surviving spouse including the augmented "deferred" marital property estate and the "elective" share right of the surviving spouse. These new substantive changes affect the law governing the property rights of spouses in Wisconsin. The 1998 Amendments to the Probate Code were initiated by the State Bar and are contained in 1997 Wisconsin Act 188. They become effective January 1, 1999. *Only* the provisions of the 1998 Amendments to the Probate Code that either directly or indirectly affect the marital property law are covered in Part III.

The Amendments to the probate Code are explained by categories. First, the new subjects added to the Probate Code. These include the requirement of survivorship by at least 120 hours and children's allowances. Second, expansion of the homestead right of the surviving spouse. Third, revisions that affect the 1984 Marital Property Act. These include the redefinition of the augmented "deferred" marital property estate and the redefinition of the surviving spouse's "elective" share in the augmented "deferred" marital property estate including the procedure for filing an "elective" share claim and the procedure for satisfying that claim. Lastly, miscellaneous changes—primarily definitions. These changes in the law governing the property rights of spouses that result from the 1998 Amendments to the Probate Code make it easier to implement the law governing transfers of property at death.

Requirements of Survivorship by 120 Hours

The requirement of survivorship by 120 hours provides that if property is transferred to an individual by a statute or under a provision in a governing instrument (such as a trust, an insurance policy or retirement benefit plan) that requires the individual to survive and it is not established the individual survived by at least 120 hours, the individual is not considered to have survived and thus is not considered qualified to receive the property transfer. Exceptions to this rule are clearly specified and include an expression of a contrary intent by a decedent.

Children's Allowances

Two new provisions in the Probate Code expand the definition of the decedent's children eligible for a support allowance during and after probate administration. Such allowances will now be available to the decedent's "dependent" children. By definition a "dependent child" means: (1) a minor child of the decedent; and (2) an adult child of the decedent who was being supported by the decedent at the time of the decedent's death. In addition, the 1998 Amendment provide that if there is no surviving spouse, the decedent's children may file with the court a written selection of certain tangible personal property, which shall thereupon be transferred to the children by the personal representative. This tangible personal property selection may not include items specifically bequeathed except that normal household furniture, furnishings and appliances necessary to maintain a home may be selected. For this purpose, antiques, family heirlooms and collections which are specifically bequeathed are not considered to be normal household furniture or furnishings.

Expansion of the Homestead Right of the Surviving Spouse

The 1998 Amendments to the Probate Code expand the rules governing the right of the surviving spouse to the couple's homestead ("home"). Previously, if a spouse died without a will (intestate) and that spouse's probate estate included an interest in the couple's "home" which would not otherwise pass to the surviving spouse under the Laws of Intestacy, then the court was required to assign that interest in the "home to the surviving spouse. The surviving spouse had to pay for that assigned interest or could refuse the assignment. However, no comparable or similar provisions governed the disposition of a "home" that was owned in nonprobate form. The 1998 Amendments continued the surviving spouse's right when the decedent dies intestate to an assignment of the couple's home except that, effective January 1, 1999, the assignment is not automatic. It must be requested by the surviving spouse.

More importantly, if there is a marital property interest in the "home," the 1998 Amendments also give the surviving spouse the same right to an assignment of the "home' when there is a will or when the "home" is governed by a nonprobate transfer, unless the deceased spouse's will or nonprobate document provides for a specific transfer of the decedent's interest in the "home" to someone other than the surviving spouse. This is a significant expansion of the surviving spouse's homestead right.

The 1998 Amendments continue to include the Probate Code's prior broad definition of "home" in connection with this provision dealing with court assignment of the "home" to the surviving spouse. The definition states that "home" "means any dwelling in which the decedent had an interest and that at the time of the decedent's death the surviving spouse occupies or intends to occupy. If there are several such dwellings, anyone may be designated by the surviving spouse. "Home" includes a house, a mobile home, a duplex or multiple apartment building one unit of which is occupied by the surviving spouse and a building used in part for a dwelling and in part for commercial or business purposes. "Home" includes all the surrounding land, unless the court sets off part of the land as severable from the remaining land.

Augmented Deferred Marital Property Estate

The new definition of the augmented "deferred" marital property estate establishes its composition in monetary terms. By specifying what property is included and what property is excluded and by prescribing uniform valuation rules for each type of property the meaning of the total value of the augmented "deferred" marital property estate is clarified.

By definition, the augmented "deferred" marital property estate is the total value of the spouses "deferred" marital property irrespective of where the property was acquired or where the property is currently located, including real property located in another jurisdiction. It includes property that falls within any of the following categories: (1) probate and nonprobate transfers of the decedent's "deferred" marital property; (2) decedent's gifts of "deferred" marital property made during the two years before the decedent's death; (3) "deferred" marital property of the surviving spouse.

There are certain exclusions to the augmented "deferred" marital property estate. The following are not included in the augmented "deferred" marital property estate; (1) transfers of "deferred" marital property to the extent that the decedent received full or partial consideration for the transfer in money or money's worth; (2) transfers under the U.S. Social Security system; (3) transfers of "deferred" marital property to persons other than the surviving spouse, with the written joinder or written consent of the surviving spouse; (4) transfers of "deferred" marital property to the surviving spouse of certain tangible property, including normal household furniture, furnishings and appliances necessary to maintain the home, if selected by the surviving spouse pursuant to Wisconsin's Probate Code.

Valuation rules are prescribed for each type of property included in the augmented "deferred" marital property estate. Valuation occurs on specific dates depending upon the type of property and the method of transfer.

Elective Share of Surviving Spouse

The "deferred" marital property "elective" share of the surviving spouse is intended to make sure that the surviving spouse will receive or own an equitable share of the "unclassified" property owned by the spouses. The "elective share of the surviving spouse in "deferred" marital property including the augmented "deferred" marital property estate was initially provided by the 1984 Marital Property Act to replace the elective share of one-third of the net probate estate to which the surviving spouse was entitled under the separate property system in effect in Wisconsin through December, 1985.

The "elective" share of the surviving spouse as redefined in the 1998 Amendments to the Probate Code gives the surviving spouse the right to a single, unified "elective" share in the augmented "deferred" marital property estate. Generally, this share is based upon one-half of the total value of the couple's "deferred" marital property, both probate and nonprobate, less the value of property transfers by the decedent spouse to the surviving spouse during lifetime or at death and the value of the surviving spouse's "deferred" marital property. This new single election combines the two prior elections provided for the surviving spouse in the Marital Property Act—one against the decedent spouse's probate "deferred" marital property and one against certain nonprobate "deferred" marital property transfers made by the decedent spouse.

In addition, the new definition of "elective" share in monetary terms replaces the surviving spouse's interest in each, and every item of "deferred" marital property in the decedent spouse's probate estate as provided in the 1984 Marital Property Act. Thus, under the 1998 Amendments, the "elective" share consistently applies to "deferred" marital property values of probate and nonprobate assets alike.

The new definition of an equitable share of the "unclassified" property puts a limit on the amount of the augmented "deferred" marital property estate the surviving spouse may receive. If the surviving spouse received property transfers from the decedent spouse and/or already owns a portion of the couple's combined probate and nonprobate "deferred" marital property, the "elective" share is reduced or eliminated. Similar limitations on the amount of the "elective" share were a part of the 1984 Marital Property Act, although the 1998 Amendments to the Probate Code requires consideration, of the surviving spouse's "deferred" marital property as well as the decedent's "deferred" marital property.

If the deceased spouse leaves a valid will, the surviving spouse may receive whatever the will provides and may also have a right to an "elective" share.

The surviving spouse has the right to elect an amount equal to no more than 50 percent of the augmented "deferred" marital property estate. Generally, in order to make the election, the surviving spouse must within six months after the date of the decedent's death, do all of the following: (1) file a petition for the election in the court having jurisdiction over the decedent's estate; (2) mail or deliver a copy of the petition to the personal representative, if any, of the decedent's estate; and (3) give notice in the manner prescribed by law of the time and place set for hearing the petition to any persons who may be adversely affected by the election.

Under certain circumstances an extension of time for election may be granted by the court. The surviving spouse may withdraw the petition for an election at any time before the probate court has entered the final determination of the distribution of the decedent's estate.

The right of election by or on behalf of the surviving spouse stipulates that the surviving spouse must be living in order for an election to be filed. If the surviving spouse does not personally file the election, it may be filed on the surviving spouse's behalf by the spouse's conservator, guardian, guardian *ad litem,* or by an agent of the spouse acting under power of attorney.

The right to elect a "deferred" marital property "elective" share may be waived by the surviving spouse in whole or in part. The waiver may take place before or after marriage. The waiver must be contained in an enforceable marital property agreement or in a signed document filed with the court after the decedent's death. Unless the waiver provides otherwise, a waiver of "all rights," or equivalent language, in the property or estate of a present or prospective spouse, is a waiver of all rights in the "deferred" marital property "elective" share.

Satisfaction of Deferred Marital Property Elective Share

The initial satisfaction of the "deferred" marital property "elective" share amount is made first from the following categories of property: (a) the value of all property included in the augmented "deferred" marital property estate based upon the surviving spouse's "deferred" marital property; and (b) the decedent spouse's, marital, individual, "deferred" marital or "deferred" individual property, probate and nonprobate, transferred to the surviving spouse.

If the property described above is inadequate to satisfy the "deferred" marital property "elective" share amount, the unsatisfied balance is satisfied proportionally from transfers to persons other than the surviving spouse of property included in the augmented "deferred" marital property estate.

The value of "deferred" marital property included in the augmented "deferred" marital property estate must be reduced by an equitable proportion of funeral and burial expenses, administrative expenses, other charges and fees and enforceable claims.

Miscellaneous Changes—Primarily Definitions

Augmented Deferred Marital Property Estate. Under the 1998 Amendments the augmented "deferred" marital property estate is the total value of all "unclassified property, probate and nonprobate, owned by the decedent spouse and the surviving spouse during marriage.

Deferred Individual Property. Under the 1998 Amendments to the Marital Property Act, at the first spouse's death "deferred" individual property is "unclassified" property of the decedent spouse or the surviving spouse which is not "deferred" marital property. "Deferred" individual property would have been classified as individual property if the Marital Property Act had been in effect when the property was acquired. It is not subject to the "elective" share right of the surviving spouse. Effective January 1, 1999 "would have been individual property" which previously had no special statutory name is "deferred individual property."

Deferred Marital Property. "Deferred marital property" means any property that satisfies all of the following: (1) is not classified by Chapter 766 of the Wisconsin Statues; (2) was acquired while the spouses were married; and (3) would have been classified as marital property under Chapter 766 if the property had been acquired when Chapter 766 applied. Under the 1998 Amendments to the Marital Property Act, at the first spouse's death, the couple's "unclassified" property acquired during marriage and before their determination date, which would have been marital property if the Marital Property Act had been in effect when the property was acquired, is classified as "deferred" marital property and the decedent's "deferred" marital property may be subject to the "elective" share right of the surviving spouse.

Dependent Child. For the purposes of the Probate Code's children's allowances, the 1998 Amendments define "dependent child" to mean any of the following (a) a minor child of the decedent; (b) an adult child who was being supported by the decedent at the time of the decedent's death

Governing Instrument. Under the 1998 Amendments, a "governing instrument" means a will, a deed, a trust instrument, an insurance or annuity policy, a contract, a pension, profit sharing, retirement or similar benefit plan, a marital property agreement, a beneficiary designation in specified property at death.

Elective Share Right. Under the 1998 Amendments to the Marital Property Act, the right of a surviving spouse to elect a portion of the decedent's "deferred" marital property is based upon probate and certain nonprobate "deferred" marital property of both spouses. The "elective" right is not an automatic right by operation of law. If the surviving spouse chooses to exercise her or his "elective" right, she or he must file with the court within six months of the decedent's death, a written notice that she or he is exercising her or his "elective" right in the decedent's "deferred" marital property.

Common Law Property Elective Share. Historically, the common law property right of a surviving spouse under the separate property system was to elect or claim a portion of the decedent spouse's assets, typically one-third of the decedent's net probate estate. The Marital Property Act repealed the common law property elective share and substituted the "elective" right of a surviving spouse to receive a portion of the decedent's "deferred" marital property, if the surviving spouse is entitled to it and chooses to do so.

Property. "Property means any interest, legal or equitable, in real or personal property, without distinction as to kind, including money, rights of a beneficiary under a contractual agreement, chooses in action and anything else that may be the subject of ownership.

Surviving Spouse. "Surviving spouse" means a person who was married to the decedent at the time of the decedent's death.

Appendix

Explanation of Terms

Definitions changed in the 1998 Amendments to the Probate Code are marked with an asterisk.

Administrator. A person appointed by the court to manage the estate of a decedent who died without a will. In Wisconsin, the term used is personal representative.

Adverse. Unfavorable; acting against or in a contrary direction.

Affirmative Action. A person must act or do something. A legal proceeding by which one demands or enforces one's right in a court of law.

Ambiguity. Capable of being understood in two or more possible senses. Example: If there is ambiguity in a law, litigation will be required to obtain a judicial decision on the meaning of the law as applied to a particular fact or situation.

Annual Exclusion (Federal Gift Tax). The right of a donor to make a tax-free annual gift of up to $10,000 to each of any number of donees in any given year.

Arbitrate. To submit a controversy to a person (arbitrator) who is mutually chosen to settle the differences between two parties or to make a binding decision on their dispute.

"As if" Rule. Under the Marital Property Act, "unclassified" property is treated during marriage "as if" it were the individual property of the person who acquired it. At the death of the

owner spouse, "unclassified" property must be classified. "Unclassified" property, which would have been marital property if it had been acquired after the Marital Property Act became effective, is classified as "deferred" marital property.

Asset. Any form of property that has value; property that can be used to pay debts.

Attestation Clause. A paragraph following the signature of the person whose will the document is and preceding the signatures of the witnesses to a will certifying that the will has been signed in their presence according to legal requirements.

*Augmented Marital Property Estate. Under the Marital Property Act, Augmented Marital Property Estate includes certain nonprobate transfers of "deferred" marital property to third parties as defined in the Act. If such transfers were made without the consent of the surviving spouse on or after April 4, 1984, the surviving spouse may have certain "elective" rights.

Basis. The value of property from which gains or losses are computed for income tax purposes. Usually, the original acquisition cost.

Beneficiary. Person who is named to receive property; for example through a life insurance policy, a retirement plan, a payable-on-death account, a trust or a will.

Bequeath. To transfer personal property such as cash, stocks, bonds, securities by will.

Bona Fide Purchaser. To acquire property by any means other than by gift, descent, or inheritance; to purchase in good faith; without fraud or deceit.

Breach. The breaking of a law, obligation, right, or duty.

Case Law. Law made by judicial decision on a case-by-case basis; judge-made law (in contrast with statutory law).

Certainty. Existence of objective, unquestionable proofs.

Classification of Property. Property classification rules determine ownership of property under the Wisconsin Marital Property Act. They classify property as marital property, individual property, or "unclassified" property.

Collateral. Property owned by a person which is used or pledged as security for the repayment of a loan.

Comingling. When property owned by one spouse is combined or added to property owned by the other spouse.

Common Law Disabilities. Under English common law married women were legally incapacitated in many areas of law. They did not have certain legal rights that men and unmarried women did. (Some-times called "disabilities of married women.")

Community Property System. A system of property rules. Under a community property system, each spouse shares equally the earnings and assets acquired during marriage resulting from the efforts of either or both spouses. All spousal property is presumed to be community property.

Concurrent Ownership. Ownership by two or more persons at the same time; i.e., joint tenancy, tenancy-in-common, community property.

Consideration. That which is regarded as the equivalent or return given or suffered by one person for the act or promise of another person.

Conveyance. To transfer real estate by a writing, such as a deed.

Corpus. The principal of a fund or trust—distinct from the income produced by it.

Co-signer. A person who signs a debt instrument with another person and is individually and jointly responsible for payment of the debt.

Credit. The right granted by a creditor to a debtor to defer payment of the debt for the purpose of obtaining money, property, labor, or services. Credit may be secured or unsecured.

Creditor. A person who grants credit to a debtor. One to whom a sum of money or other thing is owed by obligation or promise.

Debtor. One who owes a debt to a creditor and is obligated to repay.

Decedent. The person who has died.

Deed. Typically, a document dealing with real estate whereby ownership is transferred from one party to another party. A deed is often recorded in a specially designated place in the area where the real estate is located.

Deferred Employment Benefit Plan. An employee is entitled to receive a future benefit, such as a pension or retirement plan.

Deferred Individual Property. Under the Marital Property Act, "unclassified" property of a decedent spouse which is not "deferred" marital property.

Deferred Marital Property. Under the Marital Property Act, at the death of the owning spouse, the decedent's "unclassified" property acquired during marriage and before the determination date, which would have been marital property if the Marital Property Act had been in effect when the property was acquired, is classified as "deferred" marital property, and is subject to certain "elective" rights of the surviving spouse.

Descent. Acquisition of property by hereditary succession as defined by state succession or intestacy statutes, rather than by a will.

Determination Date. Under the Marital Property Act, the date on which the new marital property system becomes effective for a married couple in Wisconsin.

Devise. To transfer title to real property by means of a will.

Disclosure. The act of revealing, uncovering, or making information known.

Doctrine of Coverture. Under English common law, husband and wife were considered to be one legal person, and the wife's legal existence was suspended during marriage.

Doctrine of Necessaries. An English common law rule that the husband was liable for food, clothing, etc. furnished voluntarily by a creditor to him or his wife. "Necessaries" included goods and services based upon a person's circumstances. Some states now apply the rule without regard to gender.

Document of Title. A writing or document providing evidence of who has title to the property. Under a marital property system, title determines management and control rights of marital property. Under a separate property system, title determines ownership of property.

Domicile. The place of or principal permanent residence. A person can only have one domicile at a time.

Earned Income. Money paid to a person for his or her labor, for performing services for an employer.

*Elective Rights. Under the Marital Property Act, rights of a surviving spouse to elect up to one-half of the decedent's "deferred" marital property are applicable to probate property and certain nonprobate property. "Elective" rights are not automatic rights by operation of law. If the surviving spouse chooses to exercise her or his "elective" rights, she/he must file with the probate court within six months of the decedent's death, a written notice that she/he intends to exercise her/his "elective" rights in the decedent's property.

Elective Share. Historically, the common law property right of a surviving spouse under the separate property system to elect or claim a portion of the decedent spouse's assets, typically one-third of the decedent's net probate estate. The Marital

Property Act repealed the elective share and substituted the "elective" rights of a surviving spouse to receive up to one-half of the decedent's "deferred" marital property, if the surviving spouse chooses to do so.

English Common Law. The early English "unwritten law" based on principles and rules derived from usages and customs of antiquity or from judgments of courts enforcing such usages and customs. The term "common law" is still used to contrast statutory law from law as developed and applied by courts in legal areas not covered by statute.

Entitlement. To give a person a right, legal title, or claim to something by law.

Equal Access to Credit. Under the Marital Property Act, each spouse has equal management and control rights of marital property to obtain unsecured credit or credit where the item purchased is the security and the obligation is a family purpose obligation.

Equitable. Fair or just under the circumstances.

Equity. The system of legal and procedural rules and doctrines according to which justice is administered within certain limits of jurisdiction. It is often contrasted with the strictly formulated and applied rules of common law.

Estate Tax. A federal tax on the total gross taxable estate of a deceased person, less allowable deductions and the unified transfer tax credit.

Executor. The individual named in a will and appointed by the court to carry out the terms of the will. In Wisconsin, the term used is personal representative.

Family Purpose Obligation or Doctrine. A type of voluntary obligation defined by the Marital Property Act. It is characterized as a debt incurred by a spouse during marriage in the interest of the marriage and the family. Any debt incurred by a spouse during marriage is presumed to be in the interest of the marriage and of the family in the marital property system.

Feme Covert. A married woman.

Feme Sole. A woman not married.

Forced Share. That portion of an estate which a decedent's surviving spouse can claim by law under the separate property system, even if the property has been willed to another. (See Elective Share.)

Forms of Holding Property. Under the Marital Property Act, the document of title establishes whether the property is held as marital property or survivorship marital property (or in some cases, tenancy-in-common or joint tenancy). The name of the spouse or names of the spouses and the manner in which they are written on the document of title determine who has management and control rights over the marital property.

Fraud. Deceit; an intentional distortion of truth, whether by words, conduct, or concealment, which results in another being legally injured by surrendering a legal right or by parting with some valuable thing belonging to her or him due to reliance upon the false representation.

Gift Rule. Under the Marital Property Act, a managing spouse acting alone may not make a gift or gifts of marital property exceeding a total of $1,000 to any one person or organization in one calendar year without the consent of the other spouse, unless a larger gift is reasonable under the economic circumstances of the spouses.

Gift Tax. A federal tax on gifts made during the donor's lifetime, based on the right to transfer property, and payable by the donor.

Good Faith Duty. The Marital Property Act requires the managing spouse to act in a manner she or he reasonably believes to be in and not opposed to the best interests of the other spouse. The "good faith" duty requires that the management by one spouse shall not result in an advantage to the managing spouse or to the disadvantage of the other spouse.

Gross Taxable Estate. Includes everything in which the decedent is considered under tax laws to own an interest at the time of his or her death (including life insurance, joint property, and transfers made in contemplation of death or intended to take effect at or after death).

Guardian. The individual appointed by a court to have custody of a minor or incompetent person or that person's property under supervision of the court. The individual may be appointed as the guardian of the person or guardian of the property or both.

Heir. A person entitled to a share of a decedent's assets as determined by will or the state's intestacy laws.

Homestead. The land and buildings thereon occupied by the owners as a home for herself/himself and her/his family, and protected by law from some of the claims of creditors.

Homestead Acquisition Rule. Under the Marital Property Act, a homestead acquired on or after January 1, 1986 is classified as survivorship marital property if the deed is made out in the names of both husband and wife and there is no indication of a different intention on the deed or transfer document.

Homestead Joinder Rule. A Wisconsin requirement that the wife and husband must join in the mortgaging, gifting, or other disposition of the family's homestead, regardless of how the property is owned by the spouses.

Implementation. To carry out; to give practical effect to.

Income Rule. Under the Marital Property Act, all income earned or accrued from employment of a spouse, and income generated by all property (individual, and "unclassified") owned by a spouse after January 1, 1986, is classified as marital property, unless a unilateral statement to reclassify unearned income from marital property to individual property is properly executed.

Incurring Spouse. The spouse who creates a debt.

Individual Property. Under the Marital Property Act, property owned by one spouse is individual property. It consists of property owned by that person before marriage or acquired by gift or by inheritance during marriage. Property may also be reclassified as individual property by a marital property agreement.

Interest. A right, title, or legal share in something.

Intestate/Intestacy. A person who dies without a valid will; the condition of dying without a valid will is intestacy. Wisconsin's intestacy laws determine who receives the probate property of a decedent spouse who died without a valid will or when a person dies with a will which does not completely dispose of all of that person's probate property.

Involuntary Obligation. An obligation resulting from a tort (a negligent or intentional act) such as auto accident damages or a tax or similar obligation.

Issue. Children, grandchildren, and other direct descendants from a common ancestor.

Joinder. A requirement that two or more persons act together for a transaction to be valid, such as both spouses must sign a deed for the transfer of a homestead.

Joint Account. Under Wisconsin statutes, a bank account owned by two or more persons which allows any party to the account to withdraw the entire proceeds from the account at any time and has survivorship rights. At the death of one owner, the surviving person or persons automatically own the proceeds in the joint account without probate.

Joint Tenants/Joint Tenancy. A form of joint ownership of property, where title is in the names of two or more people, with the right of survivorship. Upon the death of one owner, the property is owned entirely by the surviving owners automatically by operation of law, without probate.

Judicial Precedent. In states with a common law background, a court decision in one state may be used to help settle a dispute in another state, if the substantive provisions and the language in the statutes are similar in both states. A state is not required to follow a judicial precedent from another state. However, a decision by the highest court of the state is binding on future courts within that state on issues governed by state law.

Jurisdiction. The legal power, right, or authority to hear and determine a case.

Legacy. A disposition in a will of a sum of money.

Liabilities. One's pecuniary or monetary obligations or debts collectively, as opposed to "assets."

Liability. Bound or obliged by law.

Life Estate. An income interest in property for life or the right to possess and enjoy property for life.

Litigation. A law suit.

Management and Control Rights. Under the Marital Property Act, where there is a document of title the document of title to marital property determines management and control rights of spouses. This is the general rule. The exception is the special management and control rule for obtaining credit.

Managing Spouse. Under the Marital Property Act, the spouse whose name is on the document of title to marital property has the right to act alone in managing and controlling that property.

Marital Account. A new type of Wisconsin bank account available *only* to husband and wife. The account allows either spouse to withdraw the entire proceeds from the account at any time. At the death of one spouse, the surviving spouse owns one-half of the sums on deposit, and the decedent's one-half of the marital account becomes a part of the decedent's probate estate.

Marital Obligations. Under the Marital Property Act, obligations incurred after 1985 in the interest of the marriage or the family. Also known as Family Purpose Obligations. They are in contrast to nonmarital obligations.

Marital Property. Under the Marital Property Act, property acquired during marriage and after the spouse's determination date as a result of the efforts of either or both spouses is automatically owned by both spouses in equal undivided shares from the moment of acquisition.

Marital Property Agreements (Regular). Under the Marital Property Act, a written agreement signed by both spouses can be used to modify most of the provisions of the marital property system. The marital property agreement is enforceable in a court of law if it meets the requirements for a valid agreement as defined by the Act.

Marital Property Agreements (Statutory). Under the Marital Property Act, a marital property agreement form defined by statute. The statutory forms of the agreement must be used as set forth in the Act, and may not be changed in any way if the form agreement is to be effective.

Marital Property Interest. Under the Marital Property Act, the equal, undivided ownership right of a spouse in marital property or property that has a marital property component.

Misrepresentation. To represent falsely or unfairly.

Mixed Property. Under the Marital Property Act, property of spouses which has both a marital property component and a nonmarital property component.

Mixing Rule. Under the Marital Property Act, if marital property is mixed with property having any other classification (nonmarital, individual, "unclassified"), the mixing reclassifies the property as marital property unless the nonmarital property can be traced.

Nonincurring Spouse. A spouse who did *not* create a debt.

Nonmanaging Spouse. Under the Marital Property Act, the spouse whose name is *not* on the document of title to marital property and has no management or control rights over that property.

Nonmarital Obligation. Under the Marital Property Act, an obligation incurred by a spouse before marriage, before the Marital Property Act became effective (pre-Act), or before the couple's determination date (pre-determination date) or any other obligation incurred by a spouse during marriage which is not a marital or family purpose obligation.

Nonmarital Property. Consists of a spouse's "unclassified" property and individual property, under the Marital Property Act.

Nonobligated Spouse. A spouse who does not have a legal duty to pay a debt. However, under the Marital Property Act, some obligations may be satisfied by creditors from *all* marital property.

Nonprobate Property. Property which passes to a survivor by operation of law and is not subject to the probate process or affected by the terms of a will.

Nontitled Property. Property for which no document of title exists, such as household furnishings and appliances, livestock, cash, etc.

Nontitled Spouse. Under the Marital Property Act, the spouse whose name is *not* on a document of title to marital property.

Obligated Spouse. A spouse who has a legal duty to pay the debt.

Obligations. A formal and binding agreement or acknowledgement of a liability. Voluntary obligations are deliberately incurred by a person, such as opening a charge account. Involuntary obligations generally arise from a negligent act, such as a car accident or from an obligation imposed by law, such as taxes.

One Hundred Percent Rule. Under the Marital Property Act, each spouse has management and control rights over 100 percent of the marital property for the purpose of obtaining unsecured credit or where the item purchased is the security and a family purpose obligation is incurred; therefore, 100 percent of the marital property is available to satisfy this obligation. Certain business property is specifically exempt from the 100 percent rule.

Open-end Credit Plan. A creditor permits a customer to add purchases or cash advances to an account from time to time, and the debtor promises to pay the creditor either the full amount or a minimum amount with interest on the unpaid balance.

Ownership Rights. A valid claim to property. Under the Marital Property Act, classification of property determines ownership of property. This is different from the separate property system where ownership of property is determined by document of title to property.

Passive Appreciation. The increase in value of an asset caused by market or inflation forces without any effort on the part of an owner.

Payable on Death (P.O.D.). Property which is transferred without probate to the named beneficiary at the death of the property owner.

Personal Effects or Possessions. Although there is no settled meaning to these phrases, they usually include wearing apparel, personal jewelry, family heirlooms such as silver, china, furniture, portraits, all cars, stamp and coin collections, etc., and books belonging to the deceased person.

Personal Property. All property other than real property; movable property, such as corporate stocks, bonds, money, bank accounts, certificates of deposit, automobiles, boats, snowmobiles, livestock, farm machinery, business inventory.

Personal Representative. The executor or administrator of the decedent's estate.

Philosophy of Law. The body of principles underlying a given law.

Pre-Act or Predetermination Date Property. Under the Marital Property Act, "unclassified" property of spouses.

Present Interest. Now existing; begun but not ended.

Presumption. An inference as to the existence of one fact not certainly known, from the known existence of some other fact. For example, under the Marital Property Act, during the marriage all property of spouses is presumed to be marital property.

Probate. A process supervised by the court or a probate registrar during which the personal representative of the estate gathers the assets, pays the debts of the decedent and other expenses involved in closing an estate and distributes the remaining property according to the terms of a will or to those entitled to receive it under the laws of intestacy.

Probate Estate. The assets left by a person at death which are subject to probate.

Probate Property. Property of the decedent that is subject to the probate process. Under the marital property system probate property includes the decedent's individual probate property, "unclassified" probate property,and a one-half interest in marital probate property.

Prorated. Something which is divided or distributed proportionally.

Prospective. Something that will occur or apply in the future.

Public Policy Issue. The term "policy" as applied to a statute, regulations, or rule of law refers to its probable rationale, effect, tendency, or objective considered with reference to the social or political well-being of the state.

Real Property. Real estate or land including everything under it, such as mineral rights, and permanent improvements to it, such as buildings.

Reclassification of Property. Under the Marital Property Act, the classification of property may be changed intentionally by one spouse or both. Spouses acting unintentionally may also change the classification of property, for example, by mixing marital property with property of another classification so that the nonmarital property cannot be traced. (See Wisconsin "Fruits" Rule, Marital Property Agreements, Tracing Rule, Active Appreciation Rule.)

Remedy. The legal means to recover a right, or to prevent or obtain redress for a wrong.

Revoke. To repeal or rescind; to take back; to cancel.

Right. Any power or privilege vested in a person by the law.

Secured Credit. Generally collateral (shares of corporate stock, bonds, real estate) already owned by the person seeking credit is pledged as security for the loan and may be taken by the creditor to satisfy the debt, if the debtor fails to pay the debt.

Separate Property System. A system of property rules. Under a separate property system, the wage earner is the sole owner of her/his earnings and all property acquired with them. The wage earner has the exclusive right to manage and control that property. Property received by gift or inheritance is owned solely by the person who received it, and the recipient has the exclusive right to manage and control it.

Silent. Absence of mention; not mentioned in a law.

Spousal Remedies. Under the Marital Property Act, court actions to protect the interest of a nonmanaging spouse in marital property or to compensate a spouse for the other spouse's fraud, mismanagement, or waste of marital property.

Spouse/Spouses. Wife and husband who are legally married or those who are about to marry and the rules apply only after they marry. Wisconsin does not recognize the concept of "common law" marriage unless a couple moving to Wisconsin resides in a state which recognizes "common law" marriages, and the couple met all the requirements of that state regarding a "common law" marriage.

Statutory Law. A law enacted by a legislative body, such as the Wisconsin legislature or the United States Congress, which is not vetoed by the Chief Executive.

Statutory Terminable Individual Property Classification Agreement. Under the Marital Property Act, a "special" marital property agreement form designed by the state and defined by statute.

Statutory Terminable Marital Property Classification Agreement. Under the Marital Property Act, a "special" marital property agreement form designed by the state and defined by statute.

Stepped-up Value. Under the Marital Property Act, at the death of a spouse, both halves of appreciated marital property owned by the decedent and the surviving spouse receive a "stepped-up" basis equal to the fair market value of the property at the time of death.

Substantial Effort Rule. Under the Marital PropertyAct, another name for the "active appreciation" rule.

Survivorship Marital Property. Under the Marital Property Act, a special form of marital property which allows the decedent spouse's interest in marital property to pass automatically at the death of one spouse to the surviving spouse without probate.

Technicalities of Law. A point of law, detail, or procedure, rule, etc., significant to the implementation of a law.

Tenants-in-Common/Tenancy in Common. A form of joint ownership of property where the names of two or more persons are on the document of title. There is no right of survivorship. A tenant may sell or gift her/his interest at any time, and may will her/his interest at death. If there is no will, the decedent's interest in such a tenancy passes under the laws of intestacy.

Terminable Interest Rule. Under the Marital Property Act, a nonemployee spouse's marital property interest in a deferred employment benefit plan terminates at death if she/he predeceases the employee spouse.

Testate/Testacy. A person who dies and has a valid will; the condition of dying with a valid will.

Third Party. A party other than the spouses. A third party may be a person or an entity such as a corporation or a charity.

Title Management Rule. Under the Marital Property Act, a spouse holding title to marital property may manage and control that property. The exception to the general title management rule is the *100 Percent Rule.*

Titled Property. Property for which a document of title exists, such as a real estate deed, a car certificate of title, corporate stock certificate.

Titled Spouse. The spouse whose name is on the document of title.

Tort. A private or civil wrong or injury which is not based on contract; a negligent or intentional act. A common tort is the causing of injury or damage in an automobile accident.

Tort Obligation. An involuntary obligation in contrast to a voluntary contractual obligation. A special rule to satisfy a tort obligation incurred by a spouse during marriage is provided in the Marital Property Act.

Tracing Rule. Under the Marital Property Act, mixed and nonmarital property will be classified as marital property unless the nonmarital part can be traced and its classification as nonmarital property can be established.

"Unclassified" Property. Under the Marital Property Act, property owned by a married couple living in Wisconsin before Janu-

ary 1, 1986 and property owned by a married couple who lived in another state and moved to Wisconsin after 1985.

Unconscionable. A legal term which means grossly unfair as decided by a court of law.

Unconstitutional. Contrary to the constitution of a state or of the United States.

Undivided. Whole; including everything without exception.

Undivided Property Interest. Right held by two or more persons in the whole property which has not been divided or distributed. Under the Marital Property Act, undivided property interests include marital property, survivorship marital property, tenants-in-common, and joint tenancy.

Undue Influence. An improper use of persuasion which destroys another person's freedom of will and thus the person does something which she or he would not do if allowed to act freely.

Unearned Income. Income received from an investment such as interest on a bank account, a dividend from a corporate stock, or rent from real estate.

Uniform Marital Property Act. The Uniform Marital Property Act was adopted by the National Conference of Commissioners on Uniform State Laws and is available to state legislatures considering property law reform. It creates a legal system of sharing within marriage of both income and property which results from the efforts of either spouse. The system called marital property is a form of community property.

Unilaterally. A person acting alone or without the consent or approval of another person.

Unsecured Credit. A promise given to a creditor by a debtor that payment of a debt will be made without giving any right or thing of value to secure this promise.

Untitled Property. Property for which no document of title exists, such as household appliances, furniture, livestock, farm machinery.

Vested. Fixed; accrued; settled; absolute; having the character or given the rights of absolute ownership; not contingent.

Voluntary Obligation. A contractual obligation or debt incurred by choice such as a loan or purchase on credit.

Wisconsin's "Fruits" Rule. Under the Marital Property Act, a spouse who owns nonmarital (individual or "unclassified") property may unilaterally (without consent of the other spouse) reclassify post 1985 "fruits" (interest, dividends, net rents) as individual property of the owning spouse by means of a signed written statement. This right to reclassify income does not apply to earned income such as wages. The Wisconsin "fruits" rule is based on a rule from Louisiana.

Selected References

Adelman, Lynn, Hanaway, Donald, and Munts, Mary Lou. "Departures from the Uniform Marital Property Act Contained in the Wisconsin Marital Property Act." Vol. 68, *Marquette Law Review*, 1985, pp. 340–403.

Baldwin, Janice and Dyke, Don. "Wisconsin's New Marital Property Law: An Overview." Legislative Reference Bureau Information Memorandum 85–6, Madison, 1985.

Baldwin, Janice and Dyke, Don. "Wisconsin Marital Property Law: An Overview," Legislative Reference Bureau Information Memorandum 94–18, Madison, WI, 1994.

Cantwell, William. "Drafting the Uniform Marital Property Act: The Issues and Debate." Vol. 21, *Houston Law Review*, 1984, pp. 669–677.

Cantwell, William. "The Uniform Marital Property Act: Origin and Intent." Vol. 68, *Marquette Law Review*, 1985, pp. 383–389.

Comment, "Sharing Debts: Creditors and Debtors Under the Uniform Marital Property Act." Vol. 69, *Minnesota Law Review*, 1985, pp. 111–139.

Comment, "Uniform Marital Property Act: Suggested Revisions for Equality Between Spouses." Vol. 1987, *University of Illinois Law Review*, pp. 471–493.

Eisler, Riane Tennenhaus. *The Equal Rights Handbook.* New York: Avon Books, 1978.

Elanger, Howard S. and Weisberger, June Miller. "From Common Property to Community Property: Wisconsin's Marital Property Act Four Years Later." Symposium: The Continuing Evolution of American Community Property Law. Vol. 1990, *Wisconsin Law Review,* pp. 769–806.

Flexner, Eleanor. *Century of Struggle.* 2d ed. revised. Cambridge, Massachusetts: Harvard University Press, 1974.

Furrh, Daniel L. "Classification of Property Under the Uniform Marital Property Act." Vol. 37, *South Carolina Law Review,* 1986, pp. 451–488.

Goebel, Karen P., Harris, Philip E., Langer, Richard J., and Roberson, Linda. *Family Estate Planning in Wisconsin.* Madison, University of Wisconsin–Extension, 1992.

Kanowitz, Leo. *Women and the Law.* Albuquerque: University of New Mexico Press, 1969.

Kyrk, Hazel. *Economic Problems of the Family.* New York: Harper and Brothers Publishers, 1933.

Kyrk, Hazel. *The Family in the American Economy.* Chicago: The University of Chicago Press, 1953.

Langer, Richard and Roberson, Linda. *Understanding Wisconsin's Marital Property Law.* Eau Claire, Wisconsin: Professional Education Systems, Inc., 1985.

Laughrey, Nanette. "Uniform Marital Property Act: A Renewed Commitment to the American Family." Vol. 65, *Nebraska Law Review,* 1985, pp. 120–160.

Marple, Annette W. and Quillian, W. Reed, Jr. "UMPA for Texas," Vol. 47, *Texas Bar Journal,* 1984, pp. 906–917.

McBride, Genevieve G. *On Wisconsin Women.* Madison: The University of Wisconsin Press, 1994.

Meuer, Teresa and Weisberger, June. *A Marital Property Handbook: An Introduction to Wisconsin's Marital Property System.* Second Edition, Madison: Center for Public Representation, 1989.

Mintz, Steven and Kellogg, Susan. "Recent Trends in American Family History: A Commentary Describing Dimensions of Demographic and Cultural Change." Vol. 21, *Houston Law Review*, 1984, pp. 789–799.

National Commission on the Observance of International Women's Year. . . . *To Form a More Perfect Union.* . . . Washington, D.C.: Superintendent of Documents, 1976.

National Conference of Commissioners on Uniform State Laws. *Uniform Marital Property Act.* Chicago, 1984.

Oldham, Thomas J. "Premarital Contracts Are Now Enforceable, Unless. . . ." Vol. 21, *Houston Law Review*, 1984, pp. 757–788.

Parkinson, Patrick. "Who Needs The Uniform Marital Property Act?" Vol. 55, *Cincinnati Law Review*, 1987, pp. 677–731.

Quaife, Milo M. (ed.). (Wisconsin Historical Collections Constitutional Series, 4 Vols.): *The Movement Toward Statehood*, Vol. I, 1918; *The Convention of 1846*, Vol. II, 1919; *The Struggle over Ratification*, Vol. III, 1920; *The Attainment of Statehood*, Vol. IV, 1928, The State Historical Society of Wisconsin, Madison.

Reppy, William A. Jr. "The Uniform Marital Property Act: Some Suggested Revisions for a Basically Sound Act." Vol. 21, *Houston Law Review*, 1984, pp. 679–716.

Salmon, Marylynn. *Women and the Law of Property in Early America.* Chapel Hill, The University of North Carolina Press, 1986.

State Bar of Wisconsin. *Wisconsin Statutes and Other Material Relating to Marital Property Reform.* Madison, 1985.

The President's Commission on the Status of Women. *American Women.* Washington, D.C.: Superintendent of Documents, 1963.

Thurman, Kay Ellen. "The Married Women's Property Acts." Unpublished Master's thesis, Law School, University of Wisconsin, Madison, 1966.

Volkmer, Ronald. "Spousal Property Rights At Death: Re–evaluation Of The Common Law Premises In Light Of The Proposed Uniform Marital Property Act." Vol. 17, *Creighton Law Review,* 1983, pp. 95–155.

Wadlington, Walter. "The Uniform Marital Property Act Symposium." Vol. 21, *Houston Law Review,* 1984, pp. 595–600.

Weinig, Mary Moers. "The Marital Property Act." Vol. 69, *Women Lawyers Journal,* November 1983, pp. 9–12.

Weisberger, June Miller. "The Wisconsin Marital Property Act: Highlights of the Wisconsin Experience In Developing A Model For Comprehensive Common Law Property Reform." Vol. 1, *Wisconsin Women's Law Journal,* 1985, pp. 5–68.

Weisberger, June Miller. "The Marital Property Act does not change Wisconsin's divorce law." *Wisconsin Bar Bulletin,* May 1987, pp. 14–17; 61–63.

Weisberger, June Miller. "Spousal Property Agreements: An Evolving Concept in Wisconsin and Elsewhere." Vol. 5, *Wisconsin Women's Law Journal,* 1990, pp. 43–79.

Weisberger, June Miller and Jackson, Bruce M. Jr. "Should Your State Adopt UMPA? Pro and Con." *Probate and Property,* September/October 1987, pp. 39–43.

Weitzman, Lenore J. "Legal Regulation of Marriage: Tradition and Change." Vol. 62, *California Law Review,* 1974, pp. 1169–1277.

Wellman, Richard V. "Third Party Interests Under the Uniform Marital Property Act." Vol. 21, *Houston Law Review,* 1984, pp. 717–756.

Wisconsin Governor's Commission on the Status of Women. *Real Women Real Lives*. Madison, 1978.

Wisconsin Legislative Reference Bureau. *Marital Property Act— A Compilation of Materials*. Informational Bulletin 84–IB–1, Madison, 1984.

Wisconsin Statutes, 1981–82, Chapter 765 "Marriage."

Wisconsin Statutes, 1981–82, Chapter 766, "Property Rights of Married Women."

Wisconsin Statutes, 1985–86, Chapter 766, "Property Rights of Married Persons: Marital Property."

Wisconsin Statutes, 1987–88, Chapter 766, "Property Rights of Married Persons: Marital Property."

Wisconsin Women's Council. *Wisconsin Women and the Law*. Madison, 1989.

Notes

Chapter 1

1. Kathryn F. Clarenbach, *Wisconsin Women Organize, 1960–80: Some Personal Reflections,* paper given at Women's Studies Conference, UW–Oshkosh, September 1986, p. 8.

2. *Real Women, Real Lives, Marriage, Divorce, Widowhood,* Wisconsin Governor's Commission on the Status of Women; Madison, 1978, p. 4.

3. *His . . . Hers . . . Theirs, Marital Property,* League of Women Voters of Wisconsin, Inc., Madison, 1978, p. 1.

4. *The Stateswoman,* Wisconsin Women's Network, Madison, September 1979, p. 1.

5. *Ibid.,* p. 4.

6. *Ibid.,* p. 1.

7. Letter from Anne Arneson, Task Force Coordinator, to Area Coordinators and Task Force members, October 25, 1979, Wisconsin Women's Network, Madison.

8. *The Stateswoman,* Op. cit., September 1979, p. 4.

9. *The Stateswoman,* "Network seeks capital gains," Wisconsin Women's Network, Madison, November 1982, p. 2.

10. Marian Thompson, The Annual Report of the Chair, Wisconsin Women's Network, Madison, June 1983, p. 3.

11.Carol Palmer, Chair, Executive Committee Member, Wisconsin Women's Network, Madison, January 3, 1985.

12.Roger McBain, "Volunteers helped push marital bill," *The Milwaukee Journal*, March 19, 1984, Late First Edition, p. 1.

13.Assembly Judiciary Committee, Representative Rutkowski, Chairman, *Committee Record* of Hearing held in Assembly Chambers at 10:00 A.M., January 15, 1980.

14. Connie Polzin, "Marital Property Bill Rapped," *Beaver Dam Daily Citizen*, Beaver Dam, May 1, 1981, p. 3.

15. Blanche V. Gleiss, "Marital Economic Task Force [Recommendations], *Governor's Task Forces on Women's Initiatives*, April 27, 1981, p. 1.

16. Ibid., p. 8.

17. Laura Lane, "Farm Women . . . You have Fewer Property Rights Than You Think," *Farm Journal*, June/July 1978, p. 35.

18. David Blaska, "Over the fence," *The Capital Times*, November 6, 1978, p. 21.

19. Laura Lane, "Farm couples ask: If marriage is a partnership why can't property be 'ours'?" *Farm Journal*, May 1983, p. 32.

20. Ray Mueller, "Vogel urges farm women to stand up for their rights," *Wisconsin State Farmer*, Waupaca County Publishing Company, Waupaca, October 25, 1985, p. 8.

21. Steve Schultze, "Some women don't like law," *The Milwaukee Journal*, December 29, 1985, p. 12.

22. Eileen Keerdoja, Lori Rotenberk and Patricia Johnson, "Schlafly Soldiers on Against the Feminists," *Newsweek*, February 28, 1983, p. 10.

23. Mrs. Mary Dietrich, "Disadvantages of A–200—The Marital Reform Bill," 5238 North 48th Street, Milwaukee, Wisconsin 53218.

24. Mrs. Mary Dietrich, *Eagle Forum*, form letter, May 28, 1985.

25. "Hearing: 71–page Marital Property Reform Bill AB 1090," *Wisconsin Report*, Wisconsin Report Publishing Company, Inc., Brookfield, Wisconsin, January 10, 1980, pp. 4 and 5.

26. "Marital Property Reform *Not* Needed," *Wisconsin Report*, September 22, 1983, p. 4.

27. "Urgent... Urgent... Urgent... Help Defeat the Wisconsin Marital Property Reform Bills," *Wisconsin Report*, September 22, 1983, p. 8.

28. Kaye Schultz, "State Bar lobbying protested." *The Capital Times*, Madison, April 22, 1982, p. 32.

29. "Hearing to address future of State Bar," *Wisconsin State Journal*, April 18, 1982, p. 6, Section 1.

30. Kaye Schultz, "Wisconsin Bar practices raise lawyers' hackles," *The Capital Times*, Madison, April 24, 1982, p. 19.

31. *Callaghan's Official Wisconsin Reports*, "Court Rules," 112 WIS.2d, Callaghan and Company, Wilmette, Illinois, 1983, p. xxv.

32. Anita Clark, Courts reporter. "Forced support of State Bar lobbying struck down," *Wisconsin State Journal*, Madison, January 23, 1986, p. 4, Section 1.

33. *Common Cause in Wisconsin Newsletter*, Madison, April 1988, pp. 2–3.

34. Arthur L. SRB, "Property reform called 'bill of decade,'" *The Capital Times*, January 15, 1980, p. 27.

35. The Associated Press, "Munts' community–property plan has opponents," *The Capital Times*, January 16, 1980, p. 18.

36. James Bartelt, "State must deal with property reform," *Green Bay Press–Gazette*, November 30, 1980, p. A14.

37. Jane Bryant Quinn, "In most states, marriage isn't a real economic partnership," *The Capital Times* December 2, 1980, p. 39.

38. Alan D. Haas, "Equality begins at home. When it comes to liberation, homemakers just aren't making it," *The Milwaukee Journal* Sunday Magazine, February 1, 1981, pp. 26 and 27.

39. Thomas W. Still, "Bills proposed to reform property system," *Wisconsin State Journal*, June 9, 1981, Section 1, p. 5.

40. Nancy J. Stohs, "An even break: That's the goal of a new drive for marital reform," *The Milwaukee Journal*, March 18, 1983, Part 2, p. 5.

41. Linda Steiner, "2 West Bend lawyers push alternative to property bill," *The Milwaukee Journal*, May 9, 1983, Part 2, p. 3.

42. Jane Bryant Quinn, "Uniform marital property law needed," *The Capital Times*, August 18, 1983, p. 10.

43. Mrs. M. F. Willequette, "Changes in state's marital property law would create chaos," *The Green Bay Press–Gazette*, October 1, 1983, p. A14.

44. Anna Marie Lux, "Marital reform law will provide equal ownership," *Janesville Gazette*, December 12, 1984, p. 1C.

45. L. Ann Zienkiewicz, "Marital Property Act: Equal split law a year away," *Greenfield Observer*, December 13, 1984, Section 2, p. 1.

46. Ray Kenney, "New law forces move to Florida, Cudahy says," *The Milwaukee Journal* Business Section, September 1, 1985, p. 1.

47. Peg Masterson, "Property law effects feared," *Milwaukee Sentinel*, September 10, 1985, Part 4, p. 1.

48. Lynn Adelman, "Don't be so quick to pan marital law," *The Milwaukee Journal* Business Section, September 15, 1985, p. 2.

49. Pat Stenson, "Marriage partners in deed, too, Headaches await Jan. 1 startup of marital property law," *Post–Crescent*, Appleton, September 22, 1985, p. B1.

50. Pat Stenson, "Former foes unite behind 'trailer bill,'" *Post–Crescent*, Appleton, September 22, 1985, p. B1.

51. John Torinus, Jr., "Marital law reform act full of unchar ted waters," *Milwaukee Sentinel*, October 1, 1985, Part 4, p. 1.

52. Richard G. Harvey, Jr., "Why marital property law should be repealed," *Racine Journal Times*, October 13, 1985, p. 15A.

53. Lynn Adelman, "Marital law reflects partnership," *Racine Journal Times*, October 13, 1985, p. 15A.

54. Ellen J. Henningsen, "Marital property reform seen benefiting all," *Milwaukee Sentinel*, October 14, 1985, Part 1, p. 18.

55. Robert F. Klaver, Jr., "Brace yourself for a full–fledged fiasco," *The Milwaukee Journal* Business Section, October 27, 1985, p. 2.

56. Marion Stewart, "Couples Advised To Prepare Now For Marital Property Law," *Sheboygan Press*, November 5, 1985, p. 4.

57. Renee Russell, "Property law not good for women, attorney tells Round Table group," *Fond du Lac Reporter*, November 15, 1985, p. 6.

58. Michael Klein, "Complications expected on marital property law," Eau Claire *Leader–Telegram* Weekend Edition, November 16, 1985, p. 3A.

59. Steve Schultze, "Some women don't like law," *The Milwaukee Journal*, December 29, 1985, Part 1, p. 12.

60. Josephine H. Staab, "Marital–law flap vastly overblown," *The Milwaukee Journal* Business Section, January 5, 1986, p. 2.

61. Laura Lane, "*Farm Women* . . You Have Fewer Property Rights than You Think," *Farm Journal*, June/July 1978, pp. 35–36.

62. Laura Lane, "Farm couples ask: If marriage is a partnership why can't property be 'ours'?" *Farm Journal*, May 1983, pp. 32–33.

63. Karen Gobel, "Marital Property Reform: Wisconsin Home Economists Tackle Public Policy, "*Journal of Home Economics*, Spring 1982, pp. 28–29.

64. Harva Hachten, "The New Marital Property Law," *Madison Magazine*, January 1985, pp. 26–52.

65. Milton E. Neshek and Robert V. Conover, "What's yours is mine, What's mine is yours," *AgVenture*, The Wisconsin Farm Bureau Magazine, Madison, WI, January/February 1986, pp 4, 5, and 7.

66. Mary Lou Munts, "Reply to Frank Nikolay regarding Marital Property," WHA–Radio, Madison, WI, July 2, 1979.

67. Ed Hinshaw, "Editorial on marital property reform," WTMJ Radio, Milwaukee, WI, February 25, 1982.

68. WHA–TV Special, "Equal Partners: Wisconsin's New Marital Property Reform Law," *Airwaves* Magazine, Friends of WHA–TV Inc., November 1985, p. 19.

69. June Miller Weisberger, "The Wisconsin Marital Property Act: Highlights of the Wisconsin Experience in Developing a Model for Comprehensive Common Law Property Reform," *Wisconsin Women's Law Journal*, Madison, Spring 1985, p. 27.

70. *Ibid.* pp. 27–28.

71. "Republican Donald Hanaway: The man who made marital property reform nonpartisan," Editorial page, *The Capital Times*, March 12, 1984, p. 10.

72. *Wisconsin Women and Public Policy*, Family Living Education, UW Extension, Madison, Spring 1984, p. 1.

73. Richard P. Jones, "Jaronitzky fought lonely battle on prop-

244 MARRIAGE AS AN ECONOMIC PARTNERSHIP

erty bill," *The Milwaukee Journal*, March 16, 1984, Late First Edition, p. 3.

74. Remarks by Governor Anthony Earl, Marital Property Bill Signing, the Capital—April 4, 1984, *State Document Legislative Reference Bureau*, Madison.

75. Wisconsin Legislative Council Report No. 5 to the 1985 Legislature, p. 3.

76. Sentinel Madison Bureau, "Legislative conferees agree on marital property bill changes," *Milwaukee Sentinel*, 2 Star Edition, October 9, 1985. (Page number not available.)

77. Richard "Dick" Matty, *Memo*: "To All State Legislators," January 16, 1987.

78. Wisconsin Legislative Council Report No. 19 to the 1991 Legislature, p. 5.

Chapter 2

1. Flexner, Eleanor. *Century of Struggle, the Woman's Rights Movement in the United States*, 2d ed. revised, Belknap Press, 1975, p. 74.

2. Eisler, Riane Tennenhaus. *The Equal Rights Handbook*, New York: Avon Books, 1978, p. 45.

3. Flexner, *op. cit.*, p. 75.

4. *Ibid.* p. 77.

5. *Ibid.* p. 77.

6. *Ibid.* pp. 146.

7. *Ibid.* p. 148.

8. *Ibid.* p. 150–151.

9. *Ibid.* p. 155.

10. *Ibid.* p. 178.

11. *Ibid.* p. 156.

12. *Ibid.* p. 176.

13. *Ibid.* p. 298.

14. McBride, Genevieve G. *On Wisconsin Women*, The University of Wisconsin Press, Madison, 1994, pp. 290–291.

15. Thurman, Kay Ellen. "The Married Women's Property

Acts." Unpublished Master's thesis, Law School, University of Wisconsin, Madison, 1966, p. 50.

16. Flexner, *op. cit.*, p. 175.

17. League of Women Voters of the United States. *In Pursuit of Equal Rights: Women in the Seventies*, Washington, D.C., 1976, p. 2.

18. *Ibid.* p. 2.

19. *Ibid.* p. 3.

20. *Ibid.* p. 3.

21. National Commission on the Observance of International Women's Year. ". . . *To Form a More Perfect Union* . . ." U.S. Government Printing Office, Washington, D.C., 1976, p. 373.

22. League of Women Voters of the United States, *In Pursuit of Equal Rights: Women in the Seventies, op. cit,* p. 3.

23. League of Women Voters of the United States. *The National Voter*, Washington, D.C., Fall 1975, p. 6

24. *Ibid.* p. 6.

25. "Schlafly celebrates defeat of ERA," *The Capital Times*, July 1, 1982, p. 4.

26. National Commission on the Observance of International Women's Year, *op. cit.*, p. 373.

27. Chapter 529, Laws of [Wisconsin] 1921.

28. Weisberger, June Miller. "The Wisconsin Marital Property Act: Highlights of the Wisconsin Experience in Developing a Model for Comprehensive Common Law Property Reform," *Wisconsin Women's Law Journal*, University of Wisconsin Law School, Madison, Spring 1985, p. 24.

29. The Governor's Commission on the Status of Women, *Wisconsin Women and the Law*, University of Wisconsin–Extension, Madison, 1975, p. 7.

30. Chapter 94, Laws of [Wisconsin] 1975.

31. Wisconsin Statutes 1975, Chapter 246, "Property Rights of Married Women."

32. Wisconsin Statutes 1984, Chapter 766, "Property Rights of Married Persons: Marital Property."

Chapter 3

1. Black, Henry. *Black's Law Dictionary, 6th Ed.*, St. Paul: West Publishing Co., 1990, p. 276.

2. Blackstone, William. *Commentaries on the Laws of England*, (J. Chitty, editor), J. B. Lippincott and Co.: Philadelphia, 1876.

3. Quaife, Milo M. (ed.). (Wisconsin Historical Collections Constitutional Series, 4 Vols.). *The Convention of 1846*, Vol. II, pp. 747–748. The State Historical Society of Wisconsin, Madison, 1919.

4. Quaife, *op. cit., The Movement Toward Statehood*, 1918. Vol. I, p. 13.

5. Quaife, *op cit., The Struggle Over Ratification*, 1920, Vol. III, pp. 360–361.

6. *Ibid.* p. 603.

7. *Ibid.* p. 465.

8. *Ibid.* p. 277.

9. *Ibid.* pp. 603–604.

10. Quaife, *op. cit., The Convention of 1846*, p. 631.

11. *Ibid.* p. 631.

12. Quaife, *op. cit., The Struggle Over Ratification*, p. 400.

13. *Ibid.* p. 385.

14. Quaife, *op. cit., The Convention of 1846*, p. 100.

15. Quaife, *op. cit., The Struggle Over Ratification*, pp. 667–668.

16. Quaife, *op. cit., The Movement Toward Statehood*, pp. 26–27.

17. Quaife, *op. cit., The Attainment of Statehood*, 1928, Vol. IV, pp. 56–57.

18. *Ibid.* p. 14.

19. *Ibid.* p. 15.

Chapter 4

1. Thurman, Kay Ellen: "The Married Woman's Property Acts." Master's Thesis, School of Law, University of Wisconsin, Madison, 1966, p. 41.

2. *Ibid.* p. 2.

3. *Ibid.* pp. 37–38.

4. *Ibid.* p. 63.

5. *Ibid.* p. 41.

6. *Ibid.* pp. 44–45.

7. *Ibid.* p. 47.

8. Wisconsin Statutes, Chapter 44, Laws of 1850.

9. Wisconsin Statutes 1981, Chapter 766.02.

10. *Ibid.* 766.03.

11. *Ibid.* 766.05.

12. *Ibid.* 766.06.

13. *Ibid.* 766.07.

14. *Ibid.* 766.075.

15. Wisconsin Statutes 1981, Chapter 765.

16. McGuire v. McGuire, 157 Neb. 226, 59 N.W. 2d 336 (1953), pp. 336–346.

17. Wisconsin Statutes 1981, Chapter 766.05.

18. Nelson v. MacDonald, 80 Wis. (1891), pp. 605–608.

19. Rasmussen v. Oshkosh Savings and Loan Association, 35 Wis. 2d 605, 151 N.W. 2d 730 (1966), pp. 605–614.

20. Wisconsin Statutes, Chapter 66, Laws of 1849, Section 1.

21. In re Estate of Kersten, 71 Wis. 2d 757, 239 N.W. 2d 86 (1976), pp. 757–766.

22. Muller v. Oregon, 208 U.W. 412 (1908), pp. 412–423.

23. National Commission on the Observance of International Women's Year: "*. . . To Form a More Perfect Union . . .*," Washington, D.C., 1976, p. 3.

24. *Ibid.* p. 3.

25. Wisconsin Governor's Commission on the Status of Women: *Real Women Real Lives, Marriage, Divorce, Widowhood,* Madison, 1978, p. 21.

26. Wisconsin Governor's Commission on the Status of Women: *That Old American Dream and the Reality of Why We Need Marital Property Reform,* Madison, 1977, p. 2.

27. The President's Commission on the Status of Women; *American Women,* Washington, D.C., 1963, p. 1.

28. *Ibid.* p. 7.

29. *Ibid.* p. 47.

30. *Ibid.* p. 47.

31. *Ibid.* p. 47.

32. *Ibid.* p. 2.

33. National Commission on the Observance of International Women's Year: *op. cit.*, p. 188.

34. *Ibid.* p. 113.

35. *Ibid.* p. vii.

36. *Ibid.* p. vi.

Chapter 5

National Conference of Commissioners of Uniform State Laws, *Uniform Marital Property Act*, Chicago, 1983.

The State Bar of Wisconsin. *Wisconsin Statutes and Other Materials Relating to Marital Property Rights*, Madison, 1985.

Wisconsin Statutes 1995–1996, Chapter 766: "Property Rights of Married Persons: Marital Property," and Chapters 851–879: "Probate Code."

Chapter 6

National Conference of Commissioners of Uniform State Laws, *Uniform Marital Property Act*, Chicago, 1983.

The State Bar of Wisconsin. *Wisconsin Statutes and Other Materials Relating to Marital Property Rights*, Madison, 1985.

Wisconsin Statutes 1995–1996, Chapter 766: "Property Rights of Married Persons: Marital Property," and Chapters 851–879: "Probate Code."

Chapter 7

National Conference of Commissioners of Uniform State Laws, *Uniform Marital Property Act*, Chicago, 1983.

The State Bar of Wisconsin. *Wisconsin Statutes and Other Materials Relating to Marital Property Rights*, Madison, 1985.

Wisconsin Statutes 1995–1996, Chapter 766: "Property Rights of Married Persons: Marital Property," and Chapters 851–879: "Probate Code."

Index